DREAM WALKER

ANDREW C. TURNER II

DREAM WALKER

Copyright © 2006 by Andrew C. Turner II

Scripture quotations are from
The Holy Bible, King James Version.

ISBN: 0-9774223-3-X

Published by

LIFEBRIDGE
BOOKS
P.O. BOX 49428
CHARLOTTE, NC 28277

Printed in the United States of America.

DEDICATION

To Andrew Carnegie Turner, my father
who passed from this life in 1955, and all inspiring
Dreamers, namely Miss Betty, my two daughters,
staff and my silent partner. You believed
in me when others doubted.

CONTENTS

INTRODUCTION

I am thrilled you have chosen to read this book. Why? Because I know in advance the positive impact it will have on your future.

Instead of a volume filled with 1-2-3, A-B-C formulas for instant success, my objective is to plant a message deep within your heart that changes you from the inside out. In the process, there will come a moment when the pieces of the puzzle fit together and you say, "That's me!" And your dream begins to unfold.

HOPE, RECOVERY AND STRENGTH

Let me confess that I began to write this book during a time when I was facing painful personal challenges. So the content isn't based on theory, but reality.

I know what it means to suffer setbacks, yet the Master used my emptiness to create words of hope, methods of recovery and prayers of strength. He took the greatest trying point of my life and instilled the most wonderful messages of expectation, peace and joy by providing pictures of victories while I was mired in battles of despair—images of abundance while in financial turmoil.

Thankfully, the power of the God-given vision He placed within me never died—and eventually the dream blossomed even more than I could imagine.

ELEMENTS OF PERFECTION

Dreams are fuel for your progression and are directly linked to the Creator. The Master challenges every man and woman into their destiny through a season of pulling, pushing, casting, drilling, and pressing. These elements of perfection are divine methods used to obtain your dedication, commitment and ultimate relationship with God.

Many who fail to understand this process have premature failures and never move into possessing what has been planted within them. I contend that a man without dreams is a man void of purpose, destiny and possibility. He has elected to accept the sum total of a compromise versus his divine harvest.

Visions are dreams which have been written into the mind, will and desire of a man. From their value and promise you begin to develop the backbone and perseverance to see the vision come to pass. You become a true Dream Walker, vowing never to surrender when life, family, friends, social or physical elements seek to darken that which God has placed in your spirit.

PASSION AND PURPOSE

Dreaming is not for all, since there is an extremely high price involved.

As you will discover on these pages, a dreamer such as Joseph can be misunderstood, cast into solitude, chased out of his homeland, alienated by family, sought after by illicit temptation, placed into pits or prison, and often forgotten by all—except God. You see, the Master gives dreams and sets people apart for a purpose.

You will also learn that during the times of severe crisis, a visionary uses the moments wisely, finding a higher awareness of passion and purpose in life.

A HEART-TRANSFORMING EXPERIENCE

In this book you will discover the answers to these vital questions:

- How can I know the difference between a self- willed desire and a God-given dream?
- What is the true measure of success?
- What are the positive aspects of rejection?
- What should my attitude be toward those who attempt to stifle my dream?
- How should I view the mistakes of my past?
- How will I first recognize the seed of a dream?
- Why must I learn to "see" with my ears instead of my eyes?
- Why is silence a symbol of strength rather than a sign of weakness?
- How will I find courage during times of testing?
- What guarantee do I have that my dream will become my destiny?

Are you ready for a life-changing, heart-transforming, Dream Walking experience? Read on!

– Andrew C. Turner II

CHAPTER 1

WHERE IT ALL BEGINS

A frail child lies in his cold hospital bed surrounded by fear. Since sickness is never like sunshine, the inclement weather and darkness seem to give approval to his illness. It was an unrelenting, chilling pain.

For a child, being alone in the dark speaks volumes of anxiety and concern. This fact seemed lost or insignificant in the environment which surrounded him.

West Penn Hospital's doctors and nurses knew him as an indigent. If his vital signs remained marginal or moved downward there was no apparent concern. He was not a person by name—only a chart of records.

Crying did not bring attention or relief, rather it often brought a closed door for children without finances or medical insurance. It seemed they were second class citizens to those with coverage.

The tears were always there, and he didn't know why, except his loneliness went unanswered. He was afraid of dying, and so confused.

How at the age of five could one die and understand life after death? This was an illogical assumption for a youth his age. He was too young to fully process logic, yet he knew something terrible was attacking his body and death would soon arrive. It came to his father, so perhaps it would call for him—and they would be together again.

This child's body was in its second major trauma. He watched as the skin peeled and flaked from his frail bones like the shedding of a reptile. The salt from his tears stung. The doctors said the scarlet fever was affecting his kidneys. He had just conquered a disease called rickets which had left him temporarily crippled.

Now this new feverous illness was moving in on his kidneys. He constantly thought of death, but who would say goodbye to his mother, Miss Betty, and his brother Carl. Who would say farewell to his two best friends, Bobby and Craig? What would happen to the promises and dreams if he would die now?

It may seem incomprehensible that a five year old would think of dying unless you examine both his history and destiny.

The child who was acquainted with facing the end of his life was me.

ACCEPTING THE CHALLENGE

Premature death is not acceptable when a dreamer has not yet completed his or her purpose on earth.

Your dream is defined as everything our Father has said about you. And living it requires "acquiring tools," support, character and accepting every opportunity to continually and consistently pursue and accomplish what the Lord has promised.

Dreams are costly, and walking them requires a substantial investment. Fortunately, what you commit increases in value over time.

My father, Andrew Carnegie Turner, died when I was two years of age. I missed him and wondered if by dying I would be able to regain a relationship with him.

I understand through conversations that my father was sickly, so my memories of him are nonexistent. I cannot recall his voice, or simple things like the texture of his skin. I do not remember his eye color; holding his hand or smelling his aftershave. How could I die and go to heaven and find Dad without knowing such personal information. What if I went to the other side and we didn't recognize each other?

I was so alone in that hospital bed, but to die at five was made more fearful by the worry I could not identify my earthly father in heaven.

Crying as a youth was not related to my anguish, for I learned early in life how to sustain suffering. I had, out of necessity, taught myself not to cry over personal hurt. The pain was often so pronounced and constant, that showing my feelings caused a greater strain on my already frail frame.

A PERSONAL CHOICE

The fact you are reading this book means you, like

me, have made the right decision. We are going to be "Dream Walkers"—and this is for you, not the world around you. Yes, others will benefit from your success, however, this is a personal choice.

Since you are equipped with desire, on these pages you will find the correct tools to shape your future, whether in family, business, ministry, marriage, or just in life.

PROTECTED BY "SOLDIERS"

Growing up, I had two best friends. Bobby and Craig both lived on our block in my neighborhood.

As children of meager means, we played with plastic soldiers, pretending to defend our block from others who lived down the street. These war games would prove valuable—as would the toy warriors during my hospital stay, especially when it was dark.

The plastic men of war belonged to Craig, so each night he would take them home for safe keeping, so he thought! Bobby and I had learned how to keep a soldier hidden in our pockets each night for protection without the knowledge of Craig.

As a child I was able to use the toy fighters as a defense mechanism against what I considered to be mean doctors and cruel nurses. A soldier is prepared to guard and provide you with comfort against any arising force. I learned how to sneak a soldier in my pocket as protection and recall asking my Heavenly Father to give him strength to shield me from death.

This was symbolic, since I believe every dreamer needs a fortress of defense. Whatever our calling, we often come under attack, so having a support system in place is vital. Most dreamers will face sorrow before realizing his or her objective.

MY CHAMPIONS

Fortunately, God will place Dream Walkers in our path while in the season of problems. My mother and aunt were great supporters for they possessed a power uncommon to most men and women.

My most endearing memories of these two incredible women will never be forgotten. Auntie Hattie now rests in heaven but Miss Betty—my mother—is noted for her belief in the impossible.

Long before we knew of faith centers, faith teachings and faith symposiums, these two women entered into prayer at my bedside, declaring that I would walk again and be healed.

Mother, as a widow, became a champion in my life for her positive declarations. I never talked to her about dying, but she would pray against the coming of death.

Even when I was frail and without answers, these women believed in my future. To be honest, based on my continuing pain, I could not see living past childhood. But this outlook was no match for Miss Betty's faith and determination.

Today, I am amazed at how they spoke life to the death and prison of my sick bed? I still marvel how they gathered divine strength, which I lacked, and spoke of life which was absent from my body?

As dreamers, we must realize that another champion—whether it is God alone or the Master's influence through a loved one or friend—is always fighting for our victory, even when it seems to us unreachable.

THE PROCESS

After the passing of my father, Miss Betty, as we fondly call her, knew how to instill greatness in her children.

Dreamers are often cast in the inequities of life, but never in impossibilities. Hold fast to your confidence.

Every facet of your existence is another stroke toward completion of a great work of art. Few will visualize the finished product while this work is being performed. Yet, you must know that every element of your life, however rewarding or painful, is part of the process of making you successful.

HARSH TREATMENT

My nights became weeks, and weeks turned into months, then years.

Most of my adolescence was spent in and out of one hospital, and there are multiple surgical wounds to remind me of this bitter beginning. My world consisted of painful needles and bedpans along with "mean" nurses. Both the doctors and hospital workers seemed angry with me—as if sickness was my choice.

Many years later I learned how the lack of health insurance and finances were part of the backdrop for this harsh treatment. In those days, indigent care was frowned upon—and it is still the case in many circles.

What I now know is that true dreamers—successful motivated believers—can start with meager resources or poor social foundations. Yet, thank God, it doesn't have to remain that way forever.

HOPE VERSUS DISDAIN

Looking back is essential, but going back is *deadly!*

The voices of my mother and aunt rang true against the will of seemingly negligent doctors and uncaring nurses. A force of determination from them began to move into my life at an early age—and remains to this day.

When facing cruel realities which come to steal your dreams and purpose, you will need to hold onto something. In my case, it was to grasp a solid serenity of life versus death, hope versus disdain, determination rather than a grave.

You may not encounter unkind nurses while being fatherless, yet may have jealous, envious friends, relatives or business associates who shake your determination. However, remember you are being shaped and molded for greatness.

RIDICULE AND REJECTION

I must admit, as a child there was a constant battle

between determination and pain. And I became weary in the warfare.

Society suggests, as do statistics, that poor children are likely to remain impoverished—and become poorly educated adults.

- The cripple will be ridiculed.
- The sickly will suffer.
- The fatherless will likely become angry,
  violent, socially deviant and have short lives.
- The dying simply die.

Another component to this inequity is called rejection—which we will discuss later in this book. But it must be included in our list of distractions to living a dream.

It is important to note that all great men or women, successful business executives, partners, theologians, community leaders and politicians face detours. What makes them a cut above average is the fact they discovered the tools to combat the demise of a vision.

EQUIPPED FOR A LIMITLESS FUTURE

Most people live out of their circumstances. However, you can made the decision to fly above conditions. It's the difference between *having* a dream and making the choice to *walk* you dream.

Rare are those who are willing to move forward and overcome their unfortunate beginning. Circumstances were never meant to define a life on earth. They are, rather, tools meant to lead us to a limitless, abundant life—one which is already lived out in the mind of our Creator.

God's vision is the one we were always *meant* to have, yet too many of us settle for the world's lies. Don't allow mean-spirited people to cancel your greatness; find a soldier to help you fight your battles!

"LIFE STRATEGISTS"?

In our twisted world, statistics have somehow become synonymous with genetics—and history is equated with destiny. Deep down, however, we know something is wrong with this picture.

Society is spending nearly $3 billion ever year on self-help books, workshops, CD's, seminars and lectures in a continuing effort to adjust to, accept, recognize, influence, understand, initiate and control the circumstances which bind us to lives we are clearly not enjoying.

Today, "life strategists" fill television talk shows, attempting to tell us how to find our authentic self. We buy the line that women came from Venus and men from Mars, so that some sense of understanding can exist between families—yet the divorce rate continues to climb.

A recent Gallup poll found that nearly 82% of Americans said they need to experience spiritual growth. So why isn't the church filling this need?

A recent trend for the church to reach society has been labeled "Post Modernity." In short, it seeks a means to reach and communicate community to a generation of "prosperity now" individuals who have lost a need for basic building principles of life. The next logical step is not to find something new, but to deal with that which brings a permanent fix to a prevailing question: "Can I truly live a dream or am I having a nightmare?"

No Longer Mystical

The book you are holding in your hand has been written to provide the next step for your personal growth, motivation, healing, wholeness, and a sense of stability. I am asking you to become aligned with me as a partner to unlock the doors which lead toward life and the fulfillment of dreams.

Each circumstance is part of the process—which is no longer mystical when a road map is provided. I am praying your aimless behavior or fear will no longer exist as we move forward in the arena of unlocking your mind and vision.

The true measure of success is not assessed by the neighbor next door but by the gift within.

Positive thinking behavior has no power unless you know your true value. Revelation is required to begin finding answers to those cold, lonely nights you have previously experienced.

There is an answer for the countless men, women, boys, and girls who are questioning the authenticity of life.

PAINTING YOUR SUCCESS CANVAS

Walls are established to prohibit movement into larger territories, but a successful dreamer has learned how to strategically eliminate certain boundaries in his or her life.

The number of obstacles you face usually has a direct relationship to the authority you possess. Great men and women who are destined to become dreamers never worry about what is "fair" or "equal." These are simply words, not expressions or experiences assigned to high achievers.

Your past inequity is part of the Master's dream for you, and should not be seen as a negative force. A stingy society and meager beginning should be merely strokes painted on your canvas of success.

Believers are not to become hopeless or sorrowful, living as though the future will somehow equate to their current situation.

We are dreamers who desire to dwell in the center of the Master's plans and expectations.

But we are not *ordinary* dreamers. We aren't among those who sleep. We don't surrender to the night and allow it to separate us from reality. Also, we aren't unaware, unconscious, or unmoved in our circumstances.

Like everything fashioned by the expert hand of our Master, we are extraordinary: extraordinary dreamers with extraordinary dreams, dreamed in extraordinary ways.

Again, we are not having dreams, we are *living* them. And what we envision is not constructed by our own imaginations. We do not shape them. Rather, we are shaped by them!

COPING WITH DISAPPOINTMENTS

Master craftsmen create patterns from which others cut cloth or fashion great works. Creating dreams is not your profession, for you are limited in this area. You are called Dream Walker—one who lives according to the call on his life.

I appeal to men first, for there's an urgent cry for you to reach your potential: *"But as it is written, Eye hath not seen, nor ear heard, neither have entered into the heart of man, the things which God hath prepared for them that love him"* (1 Corinthians 2:9).

Men need to realize there is more to manhood than what is observed, tangible and comfortable. Whether husband, father, brother, businessman, inventor, leader or motivational speaker, the responsibility we posses is far reaching.

Coping with disappointment is not an ethnicity issue. Many males from minority backgrounds begin with meager economic and social challenges. Majority men have challenges too, not reaching the levels of society which are expected.

Men who fail to live a dream often find means to cope with failures, including addictions, behavioral identities, abusive behavior and even bitterness.

SEARCHING FOR A PATTERN

Being a man is regulated by age, but *becoming* a man is regulated by his ability to possess his dreams. There is a significant difference and responsibility between the two.

——————— ⋀ ———————

A man desires to become accepted, but has few role models as a pattern.

Consequently his family, children, spouse, employment, education will become challenged when there is no motivator. He is also less likely to move forward beyond his hidden insecurities when trustworthy mentors are absent.

Hence, the vicious cycle of family abuse and marginal performance in his life often begins. This reoccurring sequence of unrest is not part of man's destiny—for from his beginning, man has possessed the heart of our Creator. He was formed in the very imagine and likeness of The Ultimate Dreamer, Master, Creator and giver of life.

A RIGHT RELATIONSHIP

Man was placed on this earth to have authority and power without limits. He participated in God's dream by naming every living creature. He was to walk in total dominion and power from his beginning.

So what has happened to this powerful creature? Or, more important, who is motivating man in this 21st

Century to take his rightful position. He is not only to have dreams but to walk them out through understanding and constant divine empowerment.

When connected with God and possessing a right relationship, there's no stopping man's ability. You may comment, "That's easy to say, but difficult to accomplish."

Achievers triumph because they learned that failure was nothing more than a platform for another winning opportunity.

Your beginning may not have included a hospital sick bed, but let me remind you every successful dreamer has faced high hurdles. Mediocrity is unacceptable. Set your sights on being a mentor, husband, father, brother, nephew or friend. There's no excuse to wait.

THE TRANSITION

As sons, men are one-dimensional. As a husband, however, this dimension takes various roads which few are properly equipped to travel.

Most husbands learn by frustration, trial and error. They are to be leaders, providers, bankers, role models—and have the ability to interpret spoken and unspoken gestures. In the church, they often are limited because of their inability to trust and find ongoing support during this period of transition.

The failure of most husbands is not in finances but rather not comprehending this change from the single life to being married. As a result, many new husbands have silent inner struggles which can cloud their ability to build a strong, stable family.

It is essential that husbands begin to take note of the warning signs which seek to attack hope and aspiration. The Lord has pronounced too many positive promises over your life to surrender.

Husbands you must not only regain your dreams, but find the means to begin living what is in your heart. You are the visionary of your family—and without vision the family will become blind and stumble.

Fathers are also multi–dimensional. They are to mold and shape the lives of their children. How? By:

- Identifying their various gifts.
- Interpreting their unspoken words.
- Nurturing them.
- Rewarding when deserved and correcting any behavior which could ultimately damage their future.

YOUR "CATALYST"

Society and church alike has labeled many men as dysfunctional or absent. It is true that millions of children are becoming adults without fathers. Daughters are becoming mothers without husbands and sons are becoming fathers without wives.

You are still a dreamer, complete with the ability to achieve worthy accomplishments in this lifetime. Certainly, there is a need inside for affirmation—for someone to say thanks for your contributions. Hopefully, your spouse is equipped to answer this need.

If she lacks this ability perhaps you need to remind her she is a catalyst for your vision. A spouse is the "finisher" of every outstanding man, and her value must extend beyond physical accompaniment.

Far too many husbands are living far below their potential due to the absence of spousal affirmation.

A marginal husband is a marginal father; therefore, he will raise his children in like manner. If this is not addressed it will negatively impact each of their lives.

I take issue with husbands and fathers who believe their real lives are hidden from their spouses and children. Not so.

Insightful fathers create insightful children, therefore, you must find the tools necessary so you will not destroy the emotional outlook of your sons or daughters.

We have been improperly trained to believe the silence of our children represents their ignorance, but young people are far more aware than we realize.

GIFTS TO BE CHERISHED

Fathers and husbands are in need of rest, not just sleep. An active mind is required for dreamers to *possess* their dream. This is why peaceful surroundings are necessary for the manifestation of a vision.

These truths are also for women, but allow me to expand on this from a male perspective.

At an alarming rate, men are leaving their leadership duties in the home, in society and in the church. Many will not speak openly regarding their internal frustration, yet it exists.

Too often we find the negative and expand on those issues. Let me suggest that we focus on the good in husbands and fathers and applaud them. This will make room for any correction rather than suggesting many elements of his life are worthless.

The Lord has placed valuable gifts in each husband and father and these treasures are to be cherished, not frowned upon or cast away.

THE CHALLENGES

Daughters are majestic beings and often the pride and joy of a father. And wives can be described as "adult daughters" who are seeking the approval of a husband.

Like husbands, wives also face a major transition process going from daughter to this position called *wife*. Our culture, society and religious communities are not adequately preparing young women for this dramatic moment of change. So women, like men, face many challenges in becoming what they once saw as the dream for their future.

If disappointments in the relationship are not addressed, they will continuously infect the family.

Remember, God didn't just form Adam, but also Eve. Women are part of the Master's greatest creations.

However, she will never reach her rightful position in marriage unless adequate help is provided in the areas of communication, responsibility and appreciation.

THE "DOUBT SYNDROME"

Since there are many evil forces which seek to interrupt dreamers, we need to live with basic truth and practical applications.

God's Word has been placed in your life so you will know how to proceed forward according to a divine plan. In this book we will identify the excuses for not pursuing your dream and replace them with sound principles based on the Master's Word.

Some may be leery because of the "doubt syndrome." Many of those falsehoods were placed into your hearing at birth, in church, college, marriage and even by *you!* Some of the lies to your dreams are in your heart due to disappointments, failures of marriages and other negative influences.

Regardless of their origin, the Truth stands ready to destroy the past and declare us free to live what God has placed within us. First, however, we have to have a clear understanding of dreams and what it means to live them. This will require exploration of both biblical truth and some interpretation.

THE COMMUNICATION BREAKDOWN

Man is considered God's most cherished creation, yet he has constantly troubled Him like no other creature.

We are gifted to verbally communicate, yet we are often incapable of proper communication. We are to become what God has said about us thereby completing the dreaming process.

In short, dreamers are those men and women who effectively commune with God and complete the course of action required to become what He has said—and has seen—in our lives. The process sounds simple, however, there is often a breakdown between the Divine and the dreamer. Man is gifted with the ability to talk, utilize deductive reasoning, thought and creative powers. He is a walking miracle, complete with a three-pound processor called a brain which has millions of cells.

When man maintains a relationship with God he is guaranteed to move from simply *having* a dream to *walking* the dream Conversely, iniquity will cause him to miss living his God-given vision.

THE DOMINION FACTOR

Since the Garden of Eden, man has been the target of pollution. His position has always made him the object of adversaries and this remains true today. God gave us the ability to possess or live our dreams through one word—*dominion*. As we mentioned, it is the power to live in the arena of life without limits.

Dominion is not force or brut strength. Rather, it is the ability given to man or woman to live what he or she has been given. However, possession will not come without the trying of faith, patience, sickness, marriage, ministry and life itself.

We begin to live our dreams as we understand dominion—the "gentle giant" inside a dreamer.

It is not the manipulative witchcraft behavior seen in some circles. Dominion knows how to stay balanced in God and with society. It is the fuel required to prosper a vision.

THE PLACE OF PASSION

Many still lack clarity regarding what God has said concerning their future. Each dreamer must seek to hear clearly the voice of the Almighty.

A critical method is to employ passion—that inner desire which prevails both in good times or in the storms of life. This is where your dream is housed.

Yes, a sickness or a dark marriage may have damaged you, but not your passion. What happened to this force while you were in a "down cycle" of life? You think it was lost, but not so. It was merely hidden as a treasure, not eternally lost.

You must battle your unworthiness while you are in the process of recalling your passion—so that you may dream out of your dominion. It will answer as you declare it into being.

You were created out of God's call for man, and your dreams are realized as a call for passion. That's why it should be high on the list of your personal desires.

Dreaming is *persuasive* passion, but living the dream is *aggressive* passion—which declares a desire to possess all God has spoken over and into your life.

MORE THAN MERE WORDS

Some individuals see dreams as the collection of the

things we desire and hope for. For many, they exist just out of reach, somewhere in the future or scribbled in a secret journal. You wonder, "Are they really attainable or should I walk away from them completely?"

Dreams are not to be vacated neither are the dreamers who possess them. In God, they are not just mere words etched on our minds. Dreams are His investment into our future.

THE DEFINITION

Take a minute and move what you have written in your journal and place it back into your heart. Then allow your mind to see what He has spoken concerning your future. Dreamers can live their dreams knowing they are God's promises concerning you. A dream then, for the man or woman of God is simply defined as: everything God has said about you and to you.

This definition combines our human understanding of the nature of dreams with the biblical illustration of their functions.

There are three ideas which make up our understanding of a dream.

First: We see it as a series of thoughts, images, or emotions occurring during sleep or in waking life (daydreaming).

Second: A dream is also depicted as something notable for its beauty, excellence, or enjoyable quality. One might say, for example that a Porsche is "a dream to drive."

Third: A dream is an ideal or a strongly desired goal or purpose.

31

From this perspective, a dream can be something that satisfies a wish. A child can think about becoming a fireman or a doctor one day.

———————⫠———————

As my mother prayed over my sickness, she saw me becoming a whole, healthy young man.

WHERE DO DREAMS BEGIN?

In scripture, the definition of the word translated "dream" is limited in both Hebrew and Greek as simply a set of images which occur when one is asleep. Often "dream" is used in conjunction with or interchangeably with "vision," but even in those instances, its meaning rarely changes beyond the fact that some visions happen when a person is awake.

However, the uses and functions of dreams are varied, and in some ways distinct from our human characterization of them.

Most people think dreams originate in their own imagination—whether caused by inner desires or by the late night snack—and are comprised of material from our own psyches, experiences, fears, and desires.

This is not always the case in the Bible. Some dreams *do* begin in man's own imagination, but this "ordinary" dreaming is hardly mentioned and seldom figures in the plot of most biblical narratives. More often, where dreams are referenced, their sole source or origin is linked to (and is as important as) their purpose and nature.

SYMBOLS OF A PROMISE

Concerning the nature of dreams and those mentioned in scripture, they can be plain or symbolic, and by extension, transparent or obscure. They can be images, both familiar and unfamiliar.

Dreams can be the voice of God, or even a *frightening* spirit. In Genesis 28:12-15, Jacob has a dream about a ladder which reached up to heaven. The ladder, and the angels who ascended and descended upon it, were symbols of a promise God had made to Jacob's father Isaac and his father Abraham. This might not have been clear to Jacob, but the Lord came to him in the dream and spoke plainly concerning what it all meant.

This is a rare instance in which a dream is both symbolic and plain. Usually, it is one or the other.

Some dreams are transparent and require no interpreter. For example, in Genesis 37, Joseph and his family knew what the dream of the sheaves meant. And when Joseph tells his father of a dream he has where the sun, the moon and eleven stars made obeisance to him, his father rebuked him, saying *"What is this dream that thou hast dreamed? Shall I and thy mother and thy brethren indeed come to bow down ourselves to thee to the earth?"* (Genesis 37:10).

Moreover, the envy which lived in the hearts of Joseph's brothers upon hearing the dream, indicates their understanding of them.

FROM ORACLES TO WARNINGS

Dreams have many purposes in scripture and are not mystical visions. They serve as oracles, vehicles for angels to carry out their work, counsel, warnings, and are indicators of spiritual health and harbingers of success, failure and judgment.

The image of dreams as oracles can be seen when men and women of scripture would "inquire of the Lord" and His answer would come to them by night. Isaiah said, *"With my soul have I desired thee in the night..."* (Isaiah 26:9).

King Saul knew the Lord had departed from him partly, because he states, *"...he answereth me no more, neither by prophets, nor by dreams"* (1 Samuel 28:15).

At other times, the Lord would seek out people in their sleep to speak to them. David wanted to build a house for God, and he related his desire to Nathan. The prophet told David to do what was in his heart, then scripture records, *"And it came to pass the same night, that the word of God came to Nathan..."* (1 Chronicles 17:3).

It is arguable that the answer from the Lord came to him in a dream.

BEWARE OF IMITATIONS

While dreams in the Bible are often associated with the health of our relationship with God, this is not always the case. The source or origin is as important as the content.

———⫟———

All dreams do not come from God,
or are delivered by angels.

34

The Almighty cautions His people against following after *"...dreams which ye cause to be dreamed"* (Jeremiah 29:8). He goes on to say, *"...they prophesy falsely unto you in my name; I have not sent them, saith the Lord"* (v.9).

This tells us dreams can come from someplace other than God. Job's friend Eliphaz claimed to have been given the wisdom of God in a dream (Job 4:12), but later, God criticized him for misrepresentation.

The Lord also rebuked Israel for trusting in idols who *"...have told* [them] *false dreams"* (Zechariah 10:2).

CONSIDER THE SOURCE

For our purposes, we're going to deal with the biblical image of dreams which originate with and in God. If our visions do not line up with those which have their source in the will of the Father, they will come to nought—for without Him we can do nothing.

Likewise, dreams from any other source (such as astrologers, psychics, well meaning but misguided friends, false teachers, and false prophets) are useless to us if they do not echo the Word and will of God.

Conversely, when they do come from the Father, nothing including death can prohibit their manifestation. Your Godly dreams leap forward in confirmation of His Word.

IT WILL LIVE

We are nothing without dreams, because if they are not present we don't have a declaration of who we are, where we're going, or what we are doing. However, it is also true that our dreams are pointless if we are just dreaming and not living them.

As the Lord places these revelations in our lives, they are to be acted upon daily. Remember, God's Word is always a finished proposition in the Spirit realm which is progressively revealed to us and the world.

Dreams then, are not possibilities to be waited on, rather promises to be banked on! God expects us to walk in everything He has said about us *today*, not doubtfully inch our way into the tomorrow He has ordained.

A SOURCE OF FAITH

Psalm 37 tells us to delight in the Lord and He will give us the desires of our hearts. In other words, loving God, means we have given Him permission to deposit dreams into us. What He places in our heart, mind and soul are promises we can walk in by faith.

David did not wonder if he would be king. This powerful man of God did not chase the throne he knew was his from his youth. Instead, he moved in wisdom, ruled others, headed armies, courageously slew Goliath and lived in "kingly ways" even before the throne became his.

A FORTRESS OF DETERMINATION

What has God placed in you to dream? Do you keep it hidden within you, or are you walking as if it is already yours?

Make sound preparations including learning how to become dedicated, consistent and filled with patience.

Dreaming is easy, walking it out requires work, sacrifice, and eventually a proven track record.

Even after many setbacks, what you envision will come alive. The problems you face may be made public, but this will help build a fortress of determination if you continuously trust the Master Dreamer.

People around you may or may not know what God has placed inside you, yet they will discern that some higher value exists—even when it is unspoken. For example, Joseph's brothers knew part of his dreams, but they also feared what they sensed.

———————⋀———————

Not everyone in your circle will celebrate what you possess, so you must guard your valuable gift.

God never deposits a dream that is to be "opened at a later date." It comes alive the moment it is spoken into your spirit and conception takes place. It may not be clear, but it is active. However, as you start living your dream, it comes into focus.

NOT BY CHANCE

Before Moses knew he would deliver Israel from Egypt, God placed him in Pharaoh's house to familiarize him with the life of leadership.

When you look back over your days, never think of valued experiences as coincidences. God is consistently in the preparation of your dreams. I pray you are beginning to receive His message. Nothing is happenstance.

Good, bad, sick, well, bankrupt or wealthy, it is all part of the plan.

———————— ⋀ ————————

Opportunities are not sought; they are presented.

This is why walking our dreams is subject to and directed by God's timing because His will for us is a part of His larger purposes for mankind. Thus, our dreams unfold at appointed times.

When God presents us with the opportunity to move toward or away from Him, it is not done in a vacuum. Other lives—often unseen—can be dramatically affected by the decisions we make.

CONSISTENT WITH THE CREATOR

Living the dream means it is an ongoing process, one that began before you were born and carries on throughout your time on earth. This consistency is seen in two ways.

First, it communicates the idea of firmness or regularity. Our faith in God should be consistent or unwavering, because He never changes. It should be free from variation or contradiction. We should be wholly committed to our dreams in inclement or fair weather, and regardless of any changes in situation or circumstances.

Second, to say a thing is consistent is to declare it is in harmony or agreement with something else. In this case, the declaration of the Word of God in our lives is true to the only yardstick by which it can be measured: itself.

Our dream-led walk must never take place outside of the requirements and restrictions of God's Word. If you are envisioning anything which is not in harmony with the desires of the Almighty for His people as written in the Holy Scriptures, you cannot live or remain in relationship with Him. How can two walk together except they agree? (Amos 3:3).

IMPASSIONED PETITIONS

The word "declare" comes from a word which means "to make clear." In this context, it denotes simply to make something known or evident.

When we declare what God has said, we make it so that others can see its evidence. For example, the Bible tells us we are *"...fearfully and wonderfully made"* (Psalm 139:14). You make this clear when you refuse to allow abusive people to perpetrate their evil will on you.

God said much to my brother and me through my mother, who we affectionately call Miss Betty. In our memory, she is often closed up in her room in our small home, pouring out prayers which would sustain us for many years following the death of my father.

It was not clear then, but I am convinced today that when Andrew Carnegie Turner, Sr., departed, God began pulling prayers from my mother for us that gave her solace and saved our lives. She would stay in her room and cry and pray until her eyes were swollen and her skin became beet red with the outpouring of her heart.

The more I listened to her pray, the more I believed God would grant her impassioned petitions. Today, much of what I am is a declaration of God's Word for me through Miss Betty's prayers.

No, being a dream walker does not mean that one is perfect in the eyes of man, but rather he or she is determined and proceeding in the will and grace of God. You are what He has declared through a divine ordinance in your life.

———————⋀———————

*Stop fighting to become what
you are not meant to be.*

Acceptance from man is great until it means rejection by Almighty God.

NECESSARY INGREDIENTS

Later, we will address specifically what is meant by God's Word and its importance in walking the dreams—as well as the difference between what He declares about us versus what the world says.

For now, it is vital that we speak what the Lord has already said concerning us. It was spoken before the foundation of the world.

Finally, declaring God's Word in our lives must be done on three levels: (1) through agreement, (2) in word and (3) in deed.

Agreement speaks of what we believe. Word has to do with what we say, and our deeds are what we do.

All three are necessary for us to effectively fulfill what God has placed within us.

MORE THAN MOTIVATION

I have written this book so you might become motivated and begin walking into the dreams you have seen—and those to come. It is not designed to tell you how to get rich or invest in the right stocks. I do, however, firmly believe that after reading these pages, you will find abundance, growth in relationships, health and healing. These are all part of the dream God intends for you.

Rather than simply motivate you, which is momentary, my aim is to *move* you, which is permanent. I also believe as you come to understand the rich life which is yours through God's Word, you will embrace, as I have, the truth that your dream—all the Lord has said concerning you—is not only your destination, but your pathway and your shield against the enemy.

When you decide to count yourself among those who are dream walkers, you have joined an elite group of heroes, on and off the pages of scripture, who do not find satisfaction until they realize every jot and tittle on the scroll of their divinely constructed future.

What an exciting journey lies ahead!

CHAPTER 2

LIVING PROOF

Death is not a popular subject among those who are alive and well. We seldom prepare for such an event and the sting from its shock lingers long after the eulogy. Instead, it is process oriented—for no one dies without experiencing at least a moment of life.

While most fear the topic of dying, few realize they are often victims many years prior to their funeral. Why? Because the death of a dreamer—and his dream—can take place without realizing what has happened. The person just gives up and surrenders without a burial.

In this chapter you will discover the "Living Proof" model for those who, for some reason or another, have not allowed death to conquer the core of their dreams.

ARMED WITH HATE

On September 11, 2001, America, the greatest country on earth, experienced a day unlike any previously known. That morning, our soil was defiled and dramatically changed.

New York City, Washington, DC, and the state of Pennsylvania became a tribunal for death at the hands of terrorists armed with hatred and disdain for our nation.

Innocent lives were lost as our cities became a battleground for what seemed to be an endless day in our history. Many of us can recall the moment as perverse, damming, hateful, bitter and halting. Yet somehow its horrific reality has begun to fade.

However, the fallout from this event is ongoing. Airline travel will never return to "business as usual" as security measures have altered our flow of travel. That day changed our lives for a season—but not forever.

You're a Target

The terrorist attacks often suffered by dreamers are aimed at their conceptual ideas and determination to move forward.

Never underestimate the power behind your dreams and aspirations since they are sent from your Master.

This being the case, they must be safely guarded.

As carriers of God's Word, all dreamers are potential targets because they possess what is valuable. This is important to grasp, otherwise you will endure the anguish of external enemies. Dream Walkers must not live with ignorance or naïve behavior as it relates to your worth.

Often, believers move through life innocently, wondering what element of their personality attracts resistance—not realizing they are chosen vessels of exceptional value.

A "LIVING DEATH"

Greatness is defined as a position or possession gained following opposition. Most noble dreamers, however, seldom address this conflict, preferring to remain focused on their vision. Rarely does an individual become exceptional without resistance—plus a measure of rejection followed by some unmerited jealousy.

If these are not countered by the Master, one will experience a "living death." This can be defined as the process of killing the mind and desire, while never touching the rest of the physical body.

Your ability and will, plus God's Word, has now become a target. Do not treat lightly the objective of your terrorist. He is out to destroy the Word. While it may feel personal, we must not *personalize* this attack.

AN AGENT OF THE ALMIGHTY

Before we examine the dreamer's response to such assaults, let's find out why the Word is so despised.

It is the manifestation of scripture through you which gives proof of why you are so hated by the enemy. As a dreamer, you are an agent of the Almighty with a high bounty on your head. So don't underestimate your value in times of spiritual warfare.

Since the deposit of the Word is not common to all, considerable forethought has gone into your selection for annihilation by the Evil One and his demons.

I trust you are beginning to realize that as a "divine

instrument" you are truly unique. However, dreamers such as you are often mislabeled and seldom valued among their peers.

Here is the good news. Believers shall triumph in every God-ordained battle.

POWERFUL WORDS

The Master Creator is Living Proof of the might of the spoken Word. In fact, He began creation with Word power. When you explore the very first chapter of the Bible, you will see how this was in full operation from the very beginning.

Creation is not the use of hands, labor, tools, construction workers, architects, engineers or planners. The bringing to life of all things, including you, is the handiwork of Word power.

The Creator began and ended His incredible work with simple but powerful words. The very essence of our universe was framed with His speech—not to Congress, to the military or to banking institutions, but to utter darkness.

Expressing His desires, the Word spoke until "Living Proof" existed. And the Master's speech produced immediate conformance.

————⋀————

Today's leaders speak, but must wait for ratification. The Word, however, is ratified the moment it is released.

46

On day six of speaking the world into existence, you and I were created and became "Living Proof" of what a dream can produce.

TURN OFF THE DARKNESS

Your ability is not dead, it is merely under attack—and sometimes darkness to the vision will occur. When night falls, set your power into motion.

What was the first element of the Creators voice? Illumination! Light was needed first to give proof of His ability. *"And God saw...that it was good"* (Genesis 1:4).

Today, you are the light of the world. A city set upon a hill that cannot be hid. One candle or ray of hope is more than sufficient to illuminate an entire football field, and your vision or dream is evidence that life abides even when darkness exists.

Immediate, measurable responses should not be the focal point of a dreamer who is searching for "Living Proof." Instead, it is like a small seedling or one blade of the crop long before harvest. So, Living Proof is the blade of life assigned to your divine deposit.

As you begin, it is essential to focus on the seed, not the entire crop.

The reason some people set unattainable goals is because they don't understand the process. And when there are no interim objectives to celebrate, we have what is commonly called "burnout." The resulting disappointment can linger until death overtakes the dream or vision. Understanding the process is essential to meet the desired goal or objective.

You are not the Master, but the gift of Him resides inside you. What gift? The gift of speech—necessary to bring life to the vision God has given.

THE "PROCESS CARRIER"

To sum up the process, speech, plus unwavering, uncompromising belief, less doubt, will produce life. [s+b<d=l]. How you believe while waiting becomes significant.

The terrorist of our soul seeks to destroy the procedure so he attacks the "process carrier." In fact, the bitter barrage aimed at a dreamer is found in scripture. The prophet Zechariah speaks of being wounded in the house of a friend (Zechariah 13:6).

Herein lies the major dread of most dreamers. Which is more deadly? Being wounded, or knowing that the foe was once called "friend"?

It is only natural to question the value of a dream when it is assailed by those who are close to us—and after such an encounter, many simply give up.

THE "MOSIAC PRINCIPLE"

To minimize the effect of being derided by those who are called friends, dreamers must learn what is called the "Mosaic Principle."

We are given "Aarons" to counter shortcomings. You see, Moses had a speech impediment, so Aaron was sent for a season as a communicator. However, when the season ended, Aaron was not able to make the transition back to his former role. Instead, he wanted control and power, and continued to negotiate long after the break from captivity. This is manipulative behavior.

There is a critical leadership lesson in this event. The Mosaic Principle simply states that you must not extend the cause of those who have limited assignments in your life. They will harm you every time.

The offence of a friend can also cause much damage to your vital organs. A heavy heart, emotional scarring and the lack of trust will make inroads into your mind. Before long, darkness will begin to overtake light and this evil will drain the life from you and your dreams.

Thank God we have Living Poof that the powerful Word will shine light and allow your vision to remain.

A CALL FOR EVIDENCE

The body of Christ is full of dreamers, yet seldom do they provide a process so others coming behind them can learn from their experience. "Living Proof" is a call for evidence among those who are alive.

Your life is the total manifestation or "complete crop" arising from what the Master has said concerning you. There is no scientific model to explore, neither will we find it in a formula or easy applications.

THE THREE TERRORS OF A DREAMER

The Evil One wages an unrelenting attack on our hopes and ambitions. We need to pay close attention to these three deadly tactics:

THE FIRST TERROR: DOUBT OR UNBELIEF

The "belief factor" of a dreamer is vital. Some believe immediately and some only after numerous battles. Thus, it is impossible to determine the time required for one to believe without doubt. It is based on the relationship between you and the Master. Your belief starts to grow when things seem impossible.

I began to believe early in my life, while experiencing much pain and rejection. In my case, I chose to have faith in the power of healing rather than the "uncaring" I felt from those in the medical profession. Perhaps this explains why the strongest believers emerge from severe circumstances.

Our faith in the impossible is shaped by trust in the Word, not people. And the first step to "Living Proof" is to trust *unconditionally* after any attack. When this is combined with belief, all things are possible.

THE SECOND TERROR: VERBAL ABUSE

Another assault on life is the power of a negative tongue. What we say can cause the dream to either flourish or wither.

Research shows the effect of verbal abuse to relationships. Old Testament scripture is also replete with illustrations of how the untamed tongue can destroy the life of a vision.

*Just as the Word brings light, an evil word
can result in darkness to the dreamer.*

In fact, the sting of a tongue—and the manner in which it is spoken—can cause a person to retreat and fail to complete his or her purpose. Even more, abusive words of rejection result in people doubting their own ability.

We should not be surprised when individuals lose their desire after repeated verbal onslaughts from leaders, peers, or family members. But remember, they are not the source of your dreams, so never allow them to be the destroyer.

Dreamers are sensitive both to words and delivery styles. This is why they love to hear the Master—whose voice is gentle and without wrath. The Almighty did not verbally abuse darkness and cause creation to unveil itself. No, He spoke softly, with compassion, and caused a great cosmic transition.

Even after Adam violated the greatest commission of creation by eating of the forbidden tree, God addressed him quietly in the cool of the garden.

Later, the Lord spoke to the prophet Elijah with *"a still small voice"* (1 Kings 19:12).

Verbal attacks tear at the value of individuals while minimizing their desire to become what the Word has declared. It is a silent killer which lingers in the minds of dreamers causing them to question their worth.

Sadly, most abuse is generational and what the father or mother expresses, so do the children.

God set the standard for communication and there was no guile. He simply said, "Let there be"—and there was.

If you are a dreamer, you already have signs of

strength, so don't allow the words of another to minimize your potential. Remember, the weapons used against you are designed to destroy your gift.

Should you be guilty of an untamed tongue, ask God to give you a new communication style And if you are being abused, seek counsel immediately. Denial only avoids the truth.

THE THIRD TERROR: REJECTION

Dreamers are not to be renegades, yet you must fully understand that being acceptable to all maybe cause for censure by God Himself. After all, our Master was not deemed to be worthy by the people of being the Chief Cornerstone, rather, He was the *"...stone which the builders rejected"* (Mark 12:10).

Rejection was given to the Son as an example of what He endured for our victory. He was shunned by men, acquainted with sorrow and felt the sting of disfavor until the end. It weighed on His mind to the point He looked up to heaven and asked, *"My God, my God, why hast thou forsaken me?"* (Mark 15:34).

However, the resurrection story lets us know He was accepted by the only One who truly counted—His Heavenly Father.

Rejection is the terror which causes humanity to act out of character:

- It is a first cousin to jealousy.
- It has no boundaries and limitations.
- It perplexes the mind and destroys determination.
- It lurks to ruin relationships.

Once a decision to reject has been made, it is seldom reversed. A dreamer should never consider turning his back on the Master. He will be lost forever without truly knowing why.

Living Proof exists so you can make it when spurned by men. The Son of God declares, *"Blessed are ye, when men...shall say all manner of evil against you"* (Matthew 5:11).

Allow rejection to bring you into a total surrender to the Master, and not to the frail desires of mankind.

THE FUTURE KING WHO WAS IGNORED

David, who became King of Israel, was both chosen and rebuffed simultaneously. Chosen by God, yet rejected by his earthly father.

The prophet Samuel was sent by the Lord to the house of Jesse—where he was to choose one of his sons to replace Saul. After seven of Jesse's sons came before him, the prophet asked Jesse, *"Are here all thy children?"* (1 Samuel 16:11).

The father had completely ignored David, who was out tending sheep in the pasture. It was as if he didn't exist. Yet, when he was called inside, Samuel was told by the Lord, *"Arise, anoint him: for this is he"* (v.12).

Even though he became king, the repudiation David experienced in his teenage years continued through adulthood. This ongoing saga should not be ignored since it made an impact on his decision-making process and desire for acceptance.

This terror played into his selection of another man's

spouse—Bathsheba—until he finally lost his most precious desire. He was barred from building the temple of worship because he continued to seek acceptance in what was forbidden and from those who were ill-equipped to provide such acceptance.

Only by finally coming to his senses and asking forgiveness was David able to regain his place in God's Kingdom. We have no record if the heart of his father or his brothers ever changed or softened toward him.

THE WORD BECAME FLESH

Dreamers and dreams provide Living Proof of the power of the Word. Here's how this was accomplished. The Bible declares, *"...the Word was made flesh, and dwelt among us"* (John 1:14).

The Master took an abstract, undefined promise, and named it Word. In a world where man was lost and without hope because of wicked behavior, doubt, sin, unbelief and immorality, this becomes the embodiment of His creative power and desire for mankind.

The fact that the Word became flesh gives credence to the "Living Proof" we are discussing.

When you think about it, the Word had to overcome many barriers to dwell among men. It had to come to life and undo the prevailing darkness and eternal damnation of mankind.

The first man, Adam, was created and fashioned from

the Word when God spoke, *"Let us make man in our image, after our likeness"* (Genesis 1:26).

The Second Adam (Jesus) was the Word manifested in flesh (1 Corinthians 15:22). It became the "Living Proof" that life and death was in the hand and mouth of our Creator.

The Word has accomplished everything it was designed to fulfill—and will not return to Him void. It has no expiration date or limitations based on time, acceptance, rejection or terror. The Word continues to go on—in you, your children and your children's children.

Because what God presents or speaks is power, it should not be treated lightly.

WALK IT OUT

By protecting and nurturing the Word, dreamers can give life to their dreams.

God's direction is often given in a series of steps He expects you to walk out in faith—even if you can't see the final destination. The drive will reveal truth far greater than the mere lines of a map. A mountain on a map is a line, but it becomes larger than life when you begin the drive.

Trust God's infallible Word. He knows the treasures which are before you —and those which are far off.

All He asks is that you keep moving forward. Your

Living Proof will never become a reality if all you do is sit and ponder its existence.

Do not over-analyze the Word. Just begin to walk into its blessings one footstep at a time.

THE PROMISE

Abraham is the father of "Living Proof." He was the recipient of the promise while in declining years. The *Word* declared, *"...thou shalt be a father of many nations"* (Genesis 17:4) and *"I will multiply thy seed as the stars of the heaven, and as the sand which is upon the sea shore"* (Genesis 22:17).

This sounds impossible, but the Word is never dependent on our understanding. It only needs obedience.

How would the promise of a child become reality when Abraham was old? Even his wife, Sarah, scoffed at the idea. But if you read his story, you'll discover how his age, his history, his lack and his inability to become a father were prevailing problems. If fact he suffered all three terrors mentioned earlier in this chapter. He faced unbelief, verbal abuse from his spouse and rejection. Yet, not one element caused him to surrender or die without having Living Proof of a Word he received.

Miss Betty, the praying mother, also scoffed at the idea. Sometimes those who pray for you will not understand the impact of their prayer.

TAKING A RISK

Perhaps you, like Abraham, are advancing in years, but still have a vision placed within you from the Lord. Don't let another day go by without moving ahead. It's not as risky as you may fear because there are no failures in His decisions for our life. The Master is never at risk, neither is His Word.

I recall leaving a prestigious engineering firm at the direction of His Word to start my own company. Many colleagues cautioned me concerning launching this new enterprise.

My partner stepped away from the venture based upon his wife's assessment of risk, leaving me to pursue the company alone.

To be successful one must never enter the arena with the Word in one hand and doubt in the other. I do not suggest that you move into business without understanding, but you must take action if the Word has given your direction.

Of course, money is required, yet its source may not be known until you take steps toward the dream.

The first contract of my new venture was not encouraging. Yet it was part of the process that later produced million dollar agreements. From this meager beginning I later opened offices in three states and received numerous awards and recognitions from the Federal Aviation Administration.

Had I hesitated without taking a risk, this experience would have never occurred, nor would the success which followed.

Moving into the Living Proof may be costly at the onset, but the lifelong experience and wealth of knowledge is beyond measure.

FOR "PERFECT PEOPLE"?

When I speak to women who are pioneers as single

parents, it is with personal understanding. Setbacks do arrive in life which will interrupt a family. Under our roof, Miss Betty successfully raised three sons without the presence of a father.

The burden of single parenting is laborious—and it is difficult to motivate children who experience lethargic lives. Contrary to the belief of some, the matter of finance is not always the issue. You simply become overwhelmed with the entire process.

Thank God, the Word was written for your situation. It is not addressed to "perfect people" who have not experienced a reverse in life, ministry, business or marriage.

Remember the story of Ruth, when a widow woman named Naomi was used to bring hope to a Moabite. More important, Naomi was a woman who suffered more than most. Her husband and two sons had died.

In this season of her life she became the Master's benchmark of instructions for Ruth, who gleaned according to Naomi's instructions.

Naomi had every right to grow bitter, but didn't. You cannot become resentful while laboring in the season God has planned—even if it means mentoring a Moabite who will marry the son of a harlot. Little did she know they would be in the divine lineage of Christ (Matthew 1:5).

Ruth and Boaz became procreators of the "Living Proof." It was directed by the Word through a broken but determined woman named Naomi.

APPLY IT!

Comprehending the nature of the Word gives us a reason for trusting in the dreams we receive from the Master. However, it is not until we understand how scripture operates that we learn how to move into the reality of our dreams.

———————⚲———————

We have the truth, yet in order for it to transform us, we have to allow it to become a part of our being.

The essence of His Word is so critical that no one book can contain its total value. The Bible is what we know to be His written message to mankind, yet His voice is not passive. What He says must be applied —today!

Dreamers never have to look for a cross to bear; it will find them. But it provides you with courage, determination and strength.

THE "LOGOS" AND "RHEMA" WORD

The Word operates on two separate levels simultaneously. The first is "logos"—His written Word. The second is "rhema"—His spoken Word.

Dreamers are to have *logos* understanding and embrace the Word in its totality—accepting it without division or exclusion.

Rhema is the power portion which contains truth, authority and might. It is the life-sustaining element of

God's promise which keeps you secure in the safety of His protection. Your dreams become *rhema* as the Lord speaks life to them.

TAKE THE LEAP!

It's not uncommon for those who have given up on their dream to tuck the desire for it deep in some unreachable corner of their heart. Unfulfilled hope and missed promises are the most painful remnants of life.

Unless the desire is restored along with the promise, the dream will eventually become aborted. The Master is pushing you into this secured area with the Word, yet it is up to you to take the first step.

Do not allow time or the voice of a "Sarah" to detour you. Take the leap! Bring Living Proof to your dormant dreams.

CHAPTER 3

PITS, PROBLEMS AND PROCESS

To most people, money and wealth are the fuel which propels the engine of their lives. Yet, there is a significant difference between the two.

Wealth is defined as the measure of worth one has obtained, while money is the instrument used to purchase goods and services. In our economic system both are highly desired, but in reality, money is a necessary "patch" for our immediate needs, but wealth or favor is an eternal well from which our dreams spring.

Dreaming is like money, however, *living* the dream moves you into a wealthy position.

Your journey has three stages. The first is a pit—as in a hole or snare. Second, there are problems which arise. Third, you cannot reach your objective without understanding the total process.

THE LUXURY LIFE

The pursuit of success through money is a dominating

force in society—and has even found its way into the church.

My experience with wealthy individuals predates ministry. By no means do I wish to diminish the Lord's work, for it is my calling, and often the labor is extremely demanding and outweighs any earthly compensation. Perhaps the Lord wanted to prepare me early in life by exposing me to a wealthy culture.

My knowledge of business practices was acquired while working for a prestigious anti-trust law firm in Washington DC. There were no limits to travel, lodging, limousines, corporate accounts, continuing education, expensive meals and three hour lunches.

Nothing was too costly. Clients were to be billed for every luxury—and they were!

Having survived bed pans, scarlet fever and a crippled childhood I somehow felt vindicated by the presence of money. It gave me a sense of relief and security.

A TEMPORARY LULL?

Time had now elapsed and corrected what to me was an unjust beginning. After all, Miss Betty had prayed for my healing and wholeness and I was no longer lying in a hospital bed. The need for the toy soldiers had long been dismissed and the pain of my past had now been replaced by money. What's more, there seemed to be an endless supply—and it was all legal!

Unlike most young men my age, the tide had turned and I was being avenged. The absence of a father and many other inequities were being corrected—so I presumed. This was the mind of an undeveloped Dream Walker.

My indigent status was replaced by full benefits with no deductions. I had no co-pay on my health care.

Truly there was justification in life, or was this a temporary lull? I could now celebrate carefree living complete with money, prestige and power—or could I? Surely a loving God would never require me to sacrifice another day or endure another process after surviving an unjust beginning.

It's His Roadway

What does a dreamer do when the Master initiates the "Pits, Problems and Process" of life a second and third time? Isn't it fair to assume that *one* survival is enough? Is it proper to label the second series as a consequence for having failed the first? What values are gained by placing a chosen dreamer into a lonely pit? Joseph certainly did not merit the journey into this horrid place.

Is the Master cruel or does He prove our worth by selecting the pathway to reach our innermost desires?

When you read the stories of high achievers, you'll find the decision to pursue a dream is theirs, but the roadway to the destination is His.

It is essential for those who have experienced success to mentor the next generation into this understanding and provide a framework for the Master to move an individual from position to position in order to establish His preeminence in the dreamer.

THREE REALITIES

I trust you have reached the stage when thoughts of surrendering or giving up are no longer a considered option. Hopefully, life's processes have matured you and you understand these three realities:

1. You know what the Lord has said concerning you.
2. The terrors of doubt, acceptance, and rejection have become silent as you no longer entertain their insidious threats.
3. The Master and you have a personal relationship that is built upon your love for Him and His for you.

Since you know how He operates, this relationship takes precedence over position or titles.

Nothing in your life has happened without a purpose. Sickness, pain, lawsuits, heartache, misery, loneliness, loss of loved ones, family, marriage, money and ministry were foundations to build upon. You are alive and well to the amazement of some, but not the Master. He knows your wealth is not tied to material means—money, prestige or fame.

You are the elect, chosen before the earth was formed.

If you truly believe this, you will depart from the deception which seeks to undermine your value. You will realize the process is not designed to destroy, but to prepare you for a higher calling.

How Long?

Have the seasons of your life ever deviated from their natural rotations? What would happen if, without forewarning, your summer became your winter and your spring your fall? How would you handle a year of summer with oppressive heat that never abates or a winter when nothing ever thaws?

I am not referring to a Tsunami which is a one-time disaster, but rather an entire shift where the Master leaves you in a negative season that does not change. You can be assured accusations would begin to fly in the community just as they did against Job—when his friends spread falsehoods against him.

As adults we are expected to adjust to the ups and downs of our existence, but what about a season where the Almighty permits the dreamer to fall prey to those who are jealous or envious of them. Their actions are cruel—as was true in the story of Joseph. He was thrown into an open pit by his brothers as a means of breaking his gift and spirit. They scoffed, *"...we shall see what will become of his dreams"* (Genesis 37:20). But Reuben said to them, *"Shed no blood, but cast him into this pit that is in the wilderness, and lay no hand upon him, that he might rid him out of their hands to deliver him to his father again"* (v.22).

All dreamers will have at least one such experience on their journey—and perhaps more.

———————⫠———————

I am convinced there is a direct
correlation between the number of setbacks
and the value of your dream.

Sadly, some refuse to follow a vision because they would rather avoid pits and problems in the process. With such an attitude they will never know the joy of triumph.

It's also important to know that trouble in the context of process help us to hold onto our dreams. Society looks for results, but they will only be temporary if we fail to go through the required stages to reach them.

MARRING YOUR PERSPECTIVE

The Master uses *every* occasion in our lives for a purpose.

Traps of life can be real, abstract, physical, mental, social and even theological. They are not like pot holes which occur following a season of inclement weather. Instead, man-made pits are designed or fashioned to blur your perspective of life. In some cases they are snares set by those who have heard of your dreams or have witnessed the hand of the Master on your life.

Strategically, these traps can be the creation of envious loved ones, business associates, friends or ministry contemporaries. Please notice they are never dug by supporters or those with like passions.

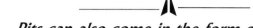

*Pits can also come in the form of verbal
negative words which find a clear pathway to a
dreamer's heart or good intentions.*

When the emotional core is penetrated, he is tempted to forfeit his aspirations.

AN OBEDIENT DREAMER

The majority of dreamers are passionate caring, sensitive beings and their hearts are open to those they love. For example, Joseph was a teenager with deep affection for his father, mother and siblings. He had no time to develop a hard, callous heart toward them and jealousy was not one of his character traits. Instead, he was a product of the Master's Hand and became a dreamer out of obedience.

In love he sought to share his gift—only to find it was not accepted. Again, the rejection process can begin when one shares dreams in a pure, unsuspecting manner. However, the innocence is often met with anger or cruel speculation.

Pit behavior is conceived in your heart and mind long before it is unleashed.

It matters not that you are highly educated or score at the top of your class. What truly matters is that the Lord allows you to dream at uncommon levels. As a result, what is natural to you becomes supernatural to those around you.

Suddenly you find yourself doing battle with those

you love and respect when your obedience to a higher calling is your only crime. You dared to live the dream!

"Is This Your Hotel?"

Relationship pits are all too real, and can be disastrous.

Recently, while in Jamaica, a young American couple and I shared a local taxi from the town, headed for our respective hotels. I greeted them, making small talk as we traveled the narrow busy street. I noticed the young man checking the items his wife had purchased at the market—to her somewhat silent disdain.

The tension between them was obvious. Finally, my assumptions became evident as we entered my hotel complex. This quiet woman asked, "Is this your hotel?

When I answered "Yes," she immediately turned to her mate and began to express her desire to change hotels. "If you really loved me we would be staying here," she blurted out.

This young man had perhaps spent all he had on this vacation thinking it would make her happy and she would be appreciative. But the woman, obviously unaware of relationship pits, began to dig one for him in my presence.

I do not know what took place before our taxicab ride, however, my heart ached for them and I was hoping to see someone extend an olive branch.

The Damage of Digging

It is counterproductive to come upon a deep hole and not look for an alternative. The Master has gifted you with many opportunities to free yourself from the entrapments of life.

In the case of my taxi ride, a pit was quickly being dug by a companion who compared love to a location. To the lady my advice would be to thank her husband for his efforts and acknowledge her appreciation, adding, "Perhaps we can stay at this hotel on our *next* visit."

My counsel to the young man would be to admit his feelings of disappointment but not internalize his bitterness. Each partner must value the other's contribution.

The paradox for this couple is much like that of Joseph. As a young man he believed his love for his family was reciprocal. However, the scheme was plotted, intentional and deliberate. His brothers knew how to deceive the dreamer, and used manipulative methods to lure him away from his father's protection. But he was never out of his Heavenly Father's sight.

A PLACE OF SAFETY

Perhaps you have been dropped into an empty place because of your God-given gifts. In the natural, you immediately want to seek justice, yet that comes later. Purpose comes first. Loved ones or enemies may have placed you there, but the Master has made provisions for your release.

You need to see your pit as a place of solace, comfort and safety. It is an experience given when the Master desires to remove you from those who fail to understand you or accept the gift you possess.

Such places are reserved for aggressive believers who have established their place in the Word and in the

Kingdom. Even if those who cast you aside seek your ultimate harm, you are protected by the Word.

A PERIOD OF TRANSITION

As unlikely as it may seem at the time, there is value to be found in the depths of the valley.

———————🝊———————

The care you will receive from above
will be better than you expect—as He provides
for you in Word and deed.

This is also a period of transition designed to bring you closer to the Almighty and a permanent transformation. The communication between you and the outside world may cease or be greatly diminished during this time, yet He is forever with you.

In my early years, my sickness was extremely confusing, but now as a survivor, I am keenly aware of the acquired strength that lies within me.

We tend to approach life and love from the view of humanity without giving thought to Divinity. Unless there is a strong personal relationship, our views are shaped to the exclusion of His plan.

My friend, it is lethal to approach a pit experience in logical thought. Divine love and application must be in operation or else one could misinterpret the lesson and even reject the Master.

How often have you accused the Lord falsely and prematurely? It's a natural thing to do. Like Joseph, it's not fair for your brothers to disrobe you and throw you into this dark abyss, knowing your only offense is expressing a dream. It seems way out of line and without merit.

SHAPING YOUR THOUGHTS

What is the purpose? What is the Master seeking to accomplish from this experience? Remember, what is dark to you is light and opportunity to Him.

Since being a dreamer is very personal, He needs you to be alone with Him. It's a season where He shapes your thoughts and strengthens your fellowship and communion with Him. He needs your undivided attention.

Use the time wisely, for you may not be there long.

REACHING FOR INSPIRATION

Pits are much like the painful points of nails, but know this: the Carpenter of Nazareth will soon be sending you a hammer and wood to build a ladder of escape. He knows both your beginning and your ability to progress.

To some, being "down in the dumps" becomes a way of life and they constantly seek sympathy. Dreamers reach for something higher—inspiration and tools to build their future.

Another key element is timing. The Lord knows how much you can handle, and when. The barriers you encounter when you are young may seem gigantic, yet He gives you the ability to overcome them. If you face the same hurdles later in life they appear much smaller because you have grown and matured.

AGENTS OF CHANGE

When you are in the pit like Joseph, it's just you and the Master. His brothers never returned to check on his well being or bring him sustenance, only to view his demise—eventually selling him to a band of spice traders headed for Egypt.

It is during this difficult time you are making the connection with your purpose. Friends and family will lack your insight, yet you are clearly hearing the voice of the Father. He is providing you with vision in this dark place.

Joseph was moving toward a palace with experience and wisdom, and he didn't allow depression, hatred and bitterness to blind him.

Those who placed you in this predicament must not be seen as your enemies, but agents of change leading you to a higher plateau.

Stop seeking validation of the dream from those who sold you into slavery. A new and better relationship awaits you.

DIVINE GIFTS

The direction you receive comes from outside your problem—not from those who are also trapped in your valley of discontent. For this reason, beware of seeking advice from individuals who are suffering with you. If they were expert pit climbers why are they with you during this season?

The Master has a specific person in mind who will lead you out of your situation. In Joseph's case it was the King of Egypt, who made him governor of the land. For you it may be a spiritual leader, a minister, loved one, business partner or a one-time friend.

Priests and ministers are divine gifts of experience, wisdom and have a shepherd's heart which is tender toward your outcome. They are chosen by the Lord, not the people. And most important, they will offer guidance that is Word and experienced based.

But remember, the Bible tells us to choose our priest wisely and *test* the prophets: *"Beloved, believe not every spirit, but try the spirits whether they are of God: because many false prophets are gone out into the world"* (1 John 4:1).

While priestly relationships are essential, not all may be in favor with your Heavenly Father. For example, if a minister is constantly condemning, it is clear he or she does not have the gift of mercy or compassion.

You will encounter several spiritual mentors as you pass through life and each has a unique approach. Some are fatherly, gentle and kind, while others may seem like correctional officers—strict and authoritative.

The Master's representative may be any of the above, but make sure there is also a spirit of love. Hopefully, he or she will understand that perhaps the season has changed and you are in a time of personal growth.

Having—and receiving—love is a critical element

since it shapes the instructions needed for your exit. An unexpected drop into a pit must be countered by compassion.

READY TO FLY

The result of all this is personal transformation—a complete metamorphous where you no longer resemble your former nature or self. This process begins in your mind as you accept the fact a value is being presented that will positively affect your life and shape your future.

However, transformation is not complete until a total submission occurs. If a caterpillar is determined to stay as he is, there will be no butterfly. The cocoon is his pit—the place of resting and yielding. Only after spending considerable time there does he become a creature of grace and beauty who can soar to the skies.

In his former state he crawled from garbage piles to dirt-filled plants, foraging to survive. Now, no longer dependent on leftovers, he is able to fly into his own desire.

This may sound like a butterfly, but it is really you, following the transition of your life.

THE NEED FOR PATIENCE

The second point of entry in this chapter is labeled "Problems." They differ from pits in that they are presented to establish knowledge, whereas pits are designed for patience.

We need to understand that patience without knowledge is counterproductive.

For example, a patient man could wait at a bus stop for hours, but a wise man will know the schedule—when they start and stop running. Standing on the curb won't make the bus arrive any quicker!

Difficulties are unavoidable as you mature and move closer to the destination of a dream.

The reason Joseph was thrown into the pit was not due to his own issues, but because of the unresolved problems of his brothers. They harbored ill feelings toward the gift of a dreamer.

Not only did they lack wisdom, they exercised a "victim mentality."

Joseph was placed in this family to provide substance, protection and territory. He was chosen by God for a season not yet seen—a future famine he would become the key to solving.

ASK FOR HELP

It's not uncommon for dreamers to be labeled as problematic. You see, the Master's nature is so active within them they often share unsuspectingly with family and friends—who may lack spiritual insight. To understand His ways with a natural mind is impossible.

The dreamer rarely knows the power residing within him. He is often the living example of "foolish things confounding the wise."

With a God-given dream you can accept an assignment which exceeds your capacity and even move in faith without knowing where the finances will come from.

Problems are not impossibilities unless *you* seek to solve them alone rather than ask for your Father's help. This can be a frustrating experience for a believer who has the innate ability to process information, form teams and resources and motivate minds to find the solution to a dilemma.

Again, problems are not sent for you to solve by yourself. Perhaps you are endowed with knowledge, head of the class and a great speaker, but don't assume you were placed on this earth to answer every question. How much better it will be when you wake up one morning with a new-found revelation called "wisdom."

THE ANSWER WAS "NO"

An associate taught me a valuable lesson which at the time seemed harsh, but in reality has proven to be a blessing.

The ministry was having some financial problems with a renovation project in our sanctuary. It began as a small undertaking, yet nothing in ministry is measured as minor, even the failures.

The church had raised the entire funds for this project only to find the carpet in the sanctuary would not match the renovations. Actually, it had become very dated and the decision was made to leave it "as is" due to the expense involved.

As the construction neared its completion we all knew that our old carpet just wouldn't harmonize with the new refurbishing, and I was facing a problem in excess of $35,000. I called an associate who had the available finances but he chose not to help us at that particular time.

After swallowing my pride, I shared my dilemma with a fellow pastor who told me of his previous challenges in building—and the denials he had received for requested funds.

Well, when I asked him if his church would loan us the money for the carpet, he replied, "No."

Here are his exact words. "If I lend you this amount it will only shift your problem from one place to another."

He also indicated that I needed to face the issue now rather than postponing it for a later date. "How uncaring," I thought. This was not personal, rather it was ministry—carpeting for the house of God!

What this pastor said next was pure revelation knowledge. He declared that the know-how to raise the money was already inside me and to obtain the funds from him would make the problem even greater. The carpet was not the issue, it was only symbolic of what was required.

Praise God, we now have the carpet that was birthed out of a problem, and it is paid in full!

THE BEST WINE

What we perceive as troubles are tools used by the Master to demonstrate His power and our favor with Him.

Jesus was once invited to a wedding feast, only to learn that a difficulty had arisen during the celebration. They had run out of wine—which the host was expected to serve to the many guests.

The Lord moved masterfully, asking that they fill the pots with water and bring them to Him.

Of course, we know the formation of wine requires the harvest of grapes, the pressing process and fermenting season. Or does it when the problem needs immediate resolution and the Master is present?

He not only turned ordinary water into wine but the latter wine was comparatively better than the former which was served at the reception.

The problem was beyond human solution. But when it reached the Lord, He took what was in their hands (water pots) and transferred the answer into His hands.

You are limited—and should only participate in the part of the difficulty you can handle. But His hands have no limitation, so the solution is in releasing your problem to the Problem Solver.

THE CHILD OF PROMISE

Difficulties may not be solved by your ability, yet they all require your confrontation—and dreamers are not to become "wimpy" in the face of challenges.

The trying of your faith works patience or knowledge,

and patience works hope and hope brings forth the child of promise.

Again, let's look at Abraham. I wonder how he felt to be "beyond age" and facing the possibility of fatherhood with a spouse who was laughing at the prospect.

Try to understand what drives a man to stand gazing at the stars and be given the burden of becoming the "father of many nations" when he has a problem becoming the father of *one* child.

God's intention for Abraham was in the form of a *promise,* not a problem.

How you view life and divine promises maybe problematic, but follow the directions of obedience. The steps are so clear until we confuse them with our human interpretations and analytical ability.

———————▲———————

Our greatest defense against being overwhelmed with troubles is to know their source.

If they are self inflicted we should realize it is lunacy to continue to operate in the same manner thinking the outcome will change.

Problems have tremendous benefits after the answer is found. When the storm subsides, in retrospect we see them as trivial, but when the lightening is flashing and the thunder rolls it is essential to view them as knowledge or empowerment.

Worry and frustration tends to shorten the life span of dreamers—and that's not beneficial to the Father, and certainly not to you.

Ask yourself how you conquered your last series of trials. Question another dreamer such as me as to how it felt to leave a prospering engineering firm for ministry.

Take a close look at the pattern of your problems and how they were solved. You'll come to the conclusion that instead of collapsing under the weight of trouble, dreamers tend to be charged with the possibility of overcoming.

Abraham "staggered not" at the promises which in his mind were stronger than Sarah's unbelief. Dreamers may have to move alone until others catch the vision and begin to submit to the Fathers will for their future.

Remember, problems are not problems until you make them personal or seek your own means to resolve them. When the Master gives you a challenge it is His duty to bring resolution. Trust in His ways and He will direct your path.

UNDERSTANDING THE PROCESS

This brings us to the final element the Master is utilizing to make you an achiever—process!

It is like patience, except you are to acquire the ability to first "wait and endure" to understand the stages you are going through. It is essential to the sustaining of life and your abundant future.

Many adults and youth alike want the benefits of dreams, yet few are willing to understand or want to submit to the process required to obtain them.

How often have you seen an ecstatic lottery winner receiving millions of dollars in a check on national television only to hear the same individual declares bankruptcy in a few short years?

Why is it the established wealthy families in America are not attracted to quick schemes or risks to gain additional wealth? What separates their riches from that of a lottery winner?

The answer is easy. Wealthy individuals *respect* wealth and the process of having it secured is ingrained into their being. They are seldom moved to spend based on emotion or become "free spending" as seen in so many lottery winners.

The recipient of a Power Ball jackpot attracts many new best friends, while the wealthy family protects old associates and relationships. The difference being that wealthy families understand the *process* of wealth.

YOUR STEPS ARE ORDERED

On Joseph's road to becoming governor of Egypt he faced family crises, false attacks and imprisonments —which were predetermined by the Master. The problems were severe but the process became second nature to Joseph.

Because of his original dream, he realized that even if a horrible event would present itself, if he remained steadfast and patient it would be removed by the supernatural power of the Almighty.

He never looked for quick answers or immediate growth but remained constant, placing one foot in front of the other. Remember, *"The steps of a good man are ordered by the Lord"* (Psalm 37:23).

Rest assured that the next victory in your life will be received and sustained through your dedication to remaining steady on the course. Do not deviate from the path even when a temptation seems profitable.

Every dreamer will experience pits and problems, yet God will reveal the process which leads to triumph.

CHAPTER 4

NO LAME EXCUSES

Failure is never really failure unless one purposely looks for a reason not to succeed. In fact, most individuals who have experienced setbacks have come to realize it is rarely permanent or fatal.

I don't wish to oversimplify failures as if there's no cause-and-effect relationship, but dreamers are cut from another cloth. They don't expect trouble to be terminal.

How do they respond to disappointment? They hurt, acknowledge what happened, assess the damages and then find a recovery plan. Seldom if ever will dreamers take center stage to publicize the "right or wrong" of the situation.

Those who consider themselves "victims" will take a lifetime seeking support for the negative effects, but positive believers will spend their days discovering ways to avoid these mishaps in the future. As a result, they will ultimately recover, have a greater insight on life and bring value to those whom they influence.

IT'S WITHIN YOUR REACH

It takes a small mind to believe that one mistake, or even several, should render you helpless or a cripple for life. Dreamers look for a ray of hope from within, not from without. Why? Because they realize success comes from what the Master places in their heart and mind.

Don't worry if the memories of your mistakes never fade; they are a valuable reminder for the future.

When individuals allow errors to slow their progress, they will often offer "lame excuses" to justify the sudden change of plans. But looking for reasons *not* to succeed is self defeating and can even shorten your life span.

Why wallow in self-pity when the promise of success is within your reach. Even more, the excuses for your condition don't make sense when you read in scripture what God has declared concerning your future.

EXTERNAL APPROVAL?

The earthly value of man is not measured by failure, rather by success. That's why you have to rise from any temporary setback or "emotional handicap" and continue pressing on. Quitting is symbolic of loss, while "hanging in there" is the sign of a winner.

The word *failure* must be defined as a temporary situation. If you are waiting for external approval, consider the risks. Not everyone is capable of offering this rare jewel called affirmation since their own life may have no acceptance. As a result, some people may pretend to support you, while secretly delighting in your downfall.

This is a very real dilemma in the 21st Century church and in business arenas. It is not uncommon to see reclusive behavior in the lives of successful men and women. While some publicly seem to "have it together," they privately suffer the pain of not being affirmed by those closest to them.

This was true at one point in the life of David when he enjoyed the blessings of God, but his family reacted in disgust at his public worship and dance (2 Samuel 6).

Rejection is one of the most crippling aspects of life, yet as dreamers we no longer have the right to offer feeble excuses for failure when hope has been placed in our hearts.

A TEMPORARY CONDITION

In a physical sense, the word "cripple" is a serious prognosis recorded after an examination of ones motor skills, muscle tissue, coordination and strength. When this is your final diagnosis, it usually means the condition is permanent.

However, when the physician pronounces a person "lame," it means a physical problem is present, but usually temporary. With time and rehabilitation, it may be reversed.

My bout with rickets made me lame for a season, but when the condition met determination powered by positive prayer, it had to give way to the Master Physician.

As it applies to dreamers, being "lame" is simply the temporary inability to move forward without the assistance of help, or some form of spiritual and mental transformation.

The person who refuses to accept this assistance, usually gives excuses—hence the term "lame excuses."

This condition has tormented outstanding men and women, however, they only became exceptional by overcoming their rationalizations.

THE VISION DIDN'T DIE

The reason I keep returning to Joseph as an example is because he personifies the dream walker. Yet, some people spend more time wondering how he landed in the pit than learning how he made his way out!

Joseph was successful in avoiding "lame excuses" because he stayed focused on the promise of God he received through the dream. Even during his unjust prison experience, the vision of what was ahead never left him.

Successful men and women have several things in common. They have strong mental motor skills combined with determination and the internal ability to know the difference between being lame or offering lame excuses.

NAVIGATING THE "GAP"

Dreamers are often faced with two extremes. First, there is the need to declare where they want to go and what they want to become. Second, they see the benefits waiting at the end of the journey.

It's a rare person who has a roadmap
and set of principles to navigate through
what I call the "gap" period of life.

This is the valley or time between knowing what your are called to become and arriving at you destination. What's in the middle? We need specific tools to propel us into mental success so we can overcome the obstacles in our path.

We must be in a position to jump the hurdles versus being overtaken by them.

There are several questions we need to ask:

- How do we effectively move forward while limping from life's disappointments?
- Is the objective attainable?
- Are there keys available to unlock future dreams when the path, both present and past, is so laced with unwanted memories, pains and experiences?
- What are dreamers to do with their hopes and aspirations when those they love have either dropped them or left them crippled?

LIVING IN LODEBAR

We can learn a great lesson from the actions of David

after he replaced Saul as King of Israel. All of the former household of the palace had either been killed or had fled. Then one day, David summoned a former servant of Saul and asked, *"Is there not yet any of the house of Saul, that I may show the kindness of God unto him?"* (2 Samuel 9:3).

The servant answered, *"Jonathan hath yet a son, which is lame on his feet"* (v.3)—his name was Mephibosheth and he was living in a place called Lodebar.

Long before, when news of the death of Saul and Jonathan reached the palace, Mephibosheth was only five years old. On hearing the disturbing report, in a panic, his nurse grabbed him and they began to flee, but the boy was dropped and became a cripple in his limbs, but not in his mind. The actions of others, even when they are of good intention, may alter the course of your life, yet they should not create permanent damage to your mind.

For years he remained in this condition, dreaming of what it would be like to return to the royal household.

David not only brought him back, he gave him land King Saul had owned. Then David announced, *"You will eat at my table continually"* (v.13).

WATCH WHERE YOU PARK!

Dreamers should never allow their minds to accept defeat since it is far more serious to be mentally crippled then physically disabled.

You may not think this is true if you try parking your car in a "handicapped" space while having a difficult day. The fine for this violation is rarely reduced.

However, I'd much rather have a physical problem than one which is mental.

I learned second hand how costly it can be to park in a handicapped space without proper verification. It was my youngest daughter who was given a summons to appear in court—where she tried to argue that the fine should be waived because she only used the special parking spot for just a few minutes.

The judge pronounced that *any* use was a violation unless she was truly handicapped.

In short, my daughter's lame excuse cost hundreds of dollars—and I was the one who had to help her foot the bill!

WHAT ABOUT YOUR PAST?

It has been said that history is the greatest enemy to one's destiny. Why is this true? Because what happened in your past can have a disabling effect on your future.

While the past has merit, we need to view it as a foundation on which failure can be built into success.

Yesterday is certainly relevant, but don't spend too much time reminiscing! Your life has so much more to offer.

Everything starts with a decision, and the most important choice you can make is not to allow your past to impair your tomorrow.

Most successful achievers, including the Lord Himself, endured incidents which attacked the very fiber of their being and sought to injure their purpose.

Perhaps you recall that of the three being crucified at Calvary, only Jesus was removed from the cross without his legs being broken.

This small fact in the New Testament is significant. The reason the bones of His legs were not damaged is because this was not the end of His story. Three days later He was to walk victoriously out of the grave and into His finest hours.

This was also to fulfill the prophecy, *"A bone of him shall not be broken"* (John 19:36).

Jesus did not have to depend on any living soul to carry Him out of the tomb, He walked out!

As a dreamer, you need to realize that no financial setback, legal battle or character assassination is capable of making you disabled for life.

"So, What's the Problem?"

If a dream or vision has divine merit, its accomplishment is based on obedience rather than ability. Yet, many have a tendency to over-complicate what has been spoken into their lives. We are intelligent in technology, medicine, engineering and other disciplines, but to what end? We have mastered the complex, yet it seems we have failed miserably at what is simple.

For example, the cell phone is no longer just a means of verbal communication; it has the ability to be a lifeline to the world—and some have enough memory to store the Old and New Testaments. Yet, few adults over 40 can successfully read email or operate a digital camera without the help of their children.

Even without reading an instruction manual, a youngster clicks a few buttons, then asks his parents, "So, what's the problem?"

Think of it. Your child—not the developing engineer or the software creator—has mastered what has confounded you. It's difficult to believe that your son or daughter, who never makes curfew and forgets to make the bed, has more skills and abilities in some areas than you! How is it that the child who thinks dirty dishes are to be left in the sink for self-cleansing, has the propensity for programming a phone (but cannot program a dishwater)?

I was having lunch with my brother and his wife in South Florida and we decided to make a video of our outing on my new digital camera, but neither of us knew how to operate it. So my sister-in-law made a long distance call to her teenage daughter who laughingly gave us step by step instructions.

I thought, "How embarrassing"—three highly educated adults using a cell phone programmed by our children to get instructions to operate a digital camera!

You may be symbolically impaired in technology, but

make the call, get help and never abandon your objective or become intimidated by the unknown.

A TIME TO WAIT

We live in a generation that doesn't seem to have the patience or the temperament to wait for dreams to come true. They want instant success. However, God's perfect timing is not always ours.

There is a huge difference between waiting and having patience.

We wait in line for airplanes, groceries, bank tellers, gas, hotel check-ins and check-outs, mail and countless other services, but often without patience. I've seen drivers move from line to line in a gas station, only to screech their wheels and leave frustrated when they couldn't reach a pump fast enough. Whose fault is it when they run out of fuel a few blocks down the street?

"HER" PERFECT WORK

The lack of patience can cripple the dream of one who is on the brink of moving into the finest days of their life.

In the New Testament, James counsels, *"...let patience have her perfect work, that ye may be perfect and entire, wanting nothing"* (James 1:4).

These words are not focused on waiting or even "time"—for most who suffer from impatience argue that they *do* wait. This may be true, yet waiting in an angry, adversarial state of mind, heart or spirit is not really patience, rather it is rebellion.

This can invite bitterness, the poison seed which slowly leads to a living grave. Patience doesn't focus on time, rather on the character of an individual.

THE WOMAN'S ROLE

It is interesting that James tells us patience should do "her" perfect work—using a feminine pronoun.

Please note that a woman was designed to *complete* Adam as his helper and be a partner in his assignment and destiny. Patience (feminine) is designed to end one's lame state, including damage to the heart which is not visible to the eye.

Being tolerant and calm brings a soothing relief to all aspects of life. This is a virtue and also a healing balm to alleviate any weak condition.

It was Miss Betty, my mother, who bathed my lame legs with oil and prayer until that which was lame and diseased became subject to her voice, her prayers and her heart.

Mother did not speak to the Lord in an angry tone because her son was suffering, rather she prayed in love—and her tears flowed out of adoration for the Master, not out of sorrow for my illness.

She patiently prayed until the Lord saw beyond my condition and looked into the purity of her heart.

My mother waited as I crawled around as a three year old, and as I wavered in my initial steps and repeated falls. But waiting alone did not bring me out of my condition, for if this were true, every such individual would eventually be delivered. It took continual patience and prayer.

Hindrances or Helps?

A lame dreamer is one who possess mental apathy and multiple excuses. You are to treasure your dreams and their value, for they come from above—and the Lord never invests in failures. He is concerned about the future.

————————⋀————————

There is no special handicap parking for lethargy.

The wheel chair for such a condition is called; defeat, depression or melancholy, and not one of these have the ability to move you through life. To the contrary, these are not means of mobility, rather hindrances which mask themselves as helps.

The Fear Factor

Unless you want to become mentally handicapped, carefully guard your mind and thoughts. There's far too much at stake.

Have you noticed there is usually a mental battle associated with a decision to move forward, versus the ease in which one can remain in a place of contentment?

We fear the unknown. In fact, your anxiety over a snake or spider is rarely based on an actual encounter with either of them. We develop apprehension from cognitive mental misinformation. In other words, our mind renders us paralyzed based on supposition, not fact.

Do not allow yourself to become incapacitated due to fear. Remember, dreamers have dominion over spiders!

THE ATTACK OF APATHY

Let me also tell you about a defeated man's best friend—apathy. It gives a person permission to justify his unwillingness to think creatively and pursue a dream following a major setback.

Ⅱ

Your indifference attacks mental mobility, slowly making inroads to your thought processes and belief systems.

I like to compare apathy and boxing. Both are contact sports, except in the first arena you can't measure the ability of your opponent or readily know when your defense tactics are having an impact. Boxing, however, permits one to see in a moment the effect of your counterattack.

Apathy may become habit forming and costly. If it is not identified and contained, it will completely consume a productive life causing it to become immobile and bankrupt.

Fighting for a dream is vastly different from natural skirmishes. Why? Because mental or spiritual battles are waged in your mind. But thankfully, you and the Master have the authority to regulate both the tone of this conflict and its length.

With a personal decision, you make a significant

attack on mental indifference every day. However, the encounter will move in your favor when your words and deeds line up with His will for you.

THE KEY TO TRANSFORMATION

It is not uncommon for visionaries to know mental discouragement, because when a mind becomes crippled, vision begins to perish. Mind-pressure will slow your progress and bring desire to a screeching halt.

Since your thoughts are at the helm of your destiny, you must take every precaution to keep them healthy.

Life has a way of finding your faults while in pursuit of promises. This is why you need to decide to leave Lodebar, that place and position of eternal brokenness (2 Samuel 9:4).

Apathy is like an ill-fated disease which appears without warning you of its intent to destroy. Its goal is to obstruct the mind and belief system without providing a wheel chair to ease your mobility.

What is the answer? The apostle Paul tells us, *"...be not conformed to this world: but be ye transformed by the renewing of your mind, that ye may prove what is that good, and acceptable, and perfect, will of God"* (Romans 12:2).

How does this change take place? It begins by *"...bringing into captivity every thought to the obedience of Christ"* (2 Corinthians 10:5).

MENTAL WARFARE

Do not allow your mind to be held under house arrest! It is a valued treasure that must be safeguarded with care and understanding.

A lame mind-set is self-destructive because it doesn't realize the value of destiny. It is a spirit which has generational curses that, if not identified and destroyed, will cause the captivity of your children and their children's children.

Doubt wants to coexist with promise, yet there's no room in your heart for both success and failure. The result is mental warfare, complete with physical and emotional unrest. In fact, many of life's physical handicaps can be directly linked to worry, anxiety, stress and other psychological disorders.

FINDING ANSWERS

Apathy has no right to be present in this new season of your life. Yes, it knows what the Master has declared concerning you before you were conceived in your mother's womb. That's why it wants to keep you right where you are—not releasing you to God's promises.

I challenge you to become a Dream Walker and find solace and strength by being alone with the Lord. Let Him reassure you that apathy will be totally defeated in the glorious season which is about to dawn.

Ask the Master to help you, and don't be afraid to call on those who also may have answers.

Is there someone in your circle who has the ability to see past your present condition? Do not allow pride to hinder you from asking. There is much to be gained from trust, teamwork and healthy relationships.

"WHERE ARE YOU?"

Adam is a clear illustration as to how the Almighty sees through our feeble excuses. The first man had been coerced into accepting fruit from the only tree which he had been told not to touch. Because of his own disobedience, he hid himself.

After noticing the forbidden tree had been disturbed, the Creator entered the garden and asked, "Adam, where are you?"

The answer he gave is the first official record of a lame excuse: Adam answered, *"I was naked; and I hid myself"* (Genesis 3:10).

The Master was focused on Adam's mental state versus his physical location since He placed man in the garden and knew each square inch—including every tree.

God knows when we disobey His command and try to use earthly things for our own purpose. As we learn in Adam's case, the results can be serious indeed.

Adam failed to take responsibility for his actions and those of his wife—and the dire consequences are still with us.

YOUR PROMISED LAND

If you're tempted to become an expert on complaining, remember the children of Israel. Because of their grumbling, they died in the desert. God waited for a new generation to arise and inherit the Promised Land.

———————— ⫰ ————————

*Achievers know that "pulling" or
coercing a group of people is self-destructive and
counterproductive, but leading them is rewarding.*

What we do with an experience is often more important than the actual experience itself. Life should be valued not because of our mistakes, but what we become as a direct result of the failure.

Don't linger in the desert forever!

TROUBLED WATERS

Jesus once confronted a lame man who was brought to the pool of Bethesda every day for 38 years, asking why he had remained in this condition so long. The man knew exactly how many years he had been there, but offered a lame excuse.

You see, many sick, blind and crippled spent their time in that location waiting for the *"moving of the water"* (John 5:3).

The Bible tells us that seasonally, an angel would come and trouble the waters—and the first one who stepped in after such an occurrence would be healed.

When Jesus asked, "Wilt thou be made whole?" the man gave this weak excuse: *"Sir, I have no man, when the water is troubled, to put me into the pool: but while I am coming, another steppeth down before me"* (v.7).

In year one, this answer would have been acceptable, but after 38 years? You would think that if someone had to feed him and bring him to the waters they could have

99

helped him in with a gentle push!

Many family traumas are generational, and I believe this was the case with this man. How lazy to ignore the need of a family member for this extended period of time?

The angel arrived periodically to disturb the water, so being late and failing to respond to his need for nearly four decades suggests someone had made him a victim.

It is not the Master's will or desire for dreamers to remain idle for a long period of time without knowing the joy of healing and liberty. So Jesus met his need with these life-changing words: *"Rise, take up thy bed, and walk"* (v.8).

This was not a rhetorical question, rather a decisive message. It tells us that transformation from lame to mobile is instant without delay or rehabilitation.

Notice the man never asked for help or assistance after hearing the command of Jesus. He was immediately healed. The lame man walked!

LIFE FOR DRY BONES!

What about you? Will you be made whole?

Recovery starts with the seed of desire and this mental change is accompanied by the will to perform.

Dreamers must remember that being lame is a temporary condition and excuses only delay and hinder any progress.

Affirmative words have power. If you pray to be made whole, make positive, Spirit-led declarations in your life daily. Why waste 38 years waiting for someone else to place you in the healing waters.

The restoration of your dream begins with proclaiming, "Yes, I want to become whole"—entire, complete.

In Ezekiel's day, a generation became so lame they were considered to be as "dry bones." But when they heard from the Master's prophet, those bones came together and stood as a great army.

Today, a voice from heaven is telling you, "No more lame excuses! Let you dream arise—and start walking."

CHAPTER 5

PERMISSION TO SPEAK

After speaking at a conference overseas, an unassuming elderly grandmother approached me following the presentation to express her personal thanks, yet immediately I could tell something was troubling her.

I had touched on the subject of relationships and she felt comfortable enough to unburden her heart and share the fact she had not been able to express her true feelings to her spouse for nearly three decades.

"Do you know how painful it is when you cannot open your mouth and speak from your heart?" she asked —and I could feel a sense of release washing over her as she continued.

She connected this inability to communicate with her anger in life, ministry and a marriage she tolerated but did not enjoy. I read between the lines that the problem was more than the lack of conversation with her spouse; there was no physical relationship.

I became saddened by her painful expressions. Here was my new question. I wondered how many couples live for years void of love, passion and intimacy due to this deadly silence. Love and passion are expressions from one's heart. It must go beyond the physical.

As our conversation continued, she pointed her family out to me in the room and I wondered, "How would they feel if they knew their mother had suffered in a marriage of silence for so long?"

Her husband was just out of range of our speaking.

Of course, my advice was that she summon the courage to bring her feelings to the surface with her spouse, because the heart of a dreamer must eventually speak what it feels.

While in that same country, I met a young man who shared how successful he had become in new business ventures, yet he confided how he actually enjoys the absence of his wife so he can find a little solitude. "I feel pressured in her presence," he reluctantly admitted.

He is just one of millions whose relationships are mired in communication conflicts.

A LEARNED BEHAVIOR

Speech is a behavior necessary for communication. As infants we began speaking by hearing sounds and voices. This mimic behavior allows children to communicate to the exclusion of sentence structures. There is no structure, just words.

Communication must go beyond speech and sound. It is a learned behavior. To that end, effective communication is constantly under refinement.

Talking involves mere words, while real communication requires awareness of others, along with an internal desire to be fully understood and appreciated.

This sharing of ideas must be mutual—without one party totally dominating and the other being submissive. Otherwise we label it manipulation or controlled, self-serving arguments.

BEYOND SILENCE

Privacy is a misunderstood concept because some tend to confuse it with a need not to communicate.

A private conversation merely suggests that all parties have a high degree of respect for each other and agree to protect the subject matter from all non–participants. More important, privacy addresses ones integrity because any violation of what has been spoken is an assault to all within the circle.

However, when this leads you into seclusion it will cloud your dreams. Why? The power of manifestation lies in your tongue. Outstanding motivators, leaders and visionaries are most valued for their impartation—not their silence, neither their seclusion.

A recluse wasn't born that way, but usually became silent following a major disruption, violation of trust or heartbreak. When this happens it prohibits inspiration to grow from within and hinders relationships from without.

When trust is broken, a Dream Walker's personality

is governed by his or her emotional and spiritual being.

PATTERNS OF THOUGHT

Most "silent dreamers" suffer from either the spirit of fear or rejection. They do not break from this reclusive stance until they begin to speak and act on the values given to them by the Father.

Hiding under a mask is not a healthy alternative. Let your determination and vision propel you to face the pain and work *through* the problem.

As a dreamer, you must begin to *measure* your communication skills, for unless you can effectively translate goals into precise patterns of thought and word, your greatest opportunities may be lost.

A TIME TO SPEAK

Effective timely communication is essential, for it will be received upon its hearing.

Your speech or communication style should flow with content and consideration of your audience. Simply put, you must know your audience to communicate effectively.

My two daughters are as different as the nearly thirteen years that separate them. The eldest is sensitive to words and expressions, and will cry easily.

Her sister, my youngest, is direct, forthright, outspoken and seldom cries. She has some of my traits, so we clash more often.

I have learned to measure my words and timing with the eldest to avoid tears, while the younger will simply state, "Are you sure this is what you want to say at this time?"

She schedules our disagreements to coincide with her moods. It actually works. Timing is everything.

"AND IT WAS GOOD"

Our vocabulary can also be divine—the result of the Master's ability to create through effective speech. We have proof of this in the clear, precise power and authority of His voice during the first six days of the formation of this world. After each event, God declared, "And it was good."

Today, the Father not only speaks Himself, but He has granted this power to every dreamer. Visionaries who are wise, prudent and clearly motivated come alive when they speak from the Father's voice.

Sadly, some have misused their tongues—resulting in poison to their own aspirations.

The mouth can produce passionate conversation or, within seconds, inflict irreparable harm which can last for decades.

Left, untamed, the tongue will ultimately cancel every promise of the Master.

If an individual cannot effectively express his dream, it will surely be lost. Likewise if a dreamer holds onto rejection, he will loose this priceless commodity.

We must somehow find permission to speak, because

"Death and life are in the power of the tongue" (Proverbs 18:21).

YOUR AUTHORITY

There is a direct correlation between the speech of a dreamer and its manifestation. Far too many lofty visions have become torpedoed by negative words.

Visionaries must lose their poor communication habits, but never their authority—which is *having* power versus *using* power.

Darkness was upon the face of the earth and had never shared its place with light until Authority spoke and said, "Let there be light." There was no argument, delay, resistance or hesitation. Light merely became as a response to the spoken Word.

ORDERLY COMMUNICATION

When a dreamer becomes silent—without sound or speech—it should be for two reasons:

1. To hear the Master's voice.
2. When additional information is being gathered—either through inspiration, facts or another person.

Creation was accomplished through structured communication so that all of humanity would recognize authority must be orderly. And if the internal life of a dreamer is without a framework, his speech will depict the same disjointed behavior.

VERBAL BATTLES?

As a dreamer, you are a prized commodity to the Creator. You have promise, purpose and destiny—and this value is enhanced by your ability to effectively speak with the Father and others who are privileged to be in your life.

Speech is not synonymous with communication for the latter builds relationships that are essential to fortifying your future, while "talk" can act to destroy it.

When an individual is damaged, or lives with emotional scar tissue, you can be sure his or her speech will affect others.

Adversities of life often launch people into verbal rampages—and dreamers are not adept at waging war in silence.

This is a learned behavior. Dreamers do not fight battles unless they have spoils or wealth.

Not every conflict requires your attention. In fact, it may be merely a distraction to keep you blinded or out of focus. Some individuals pull others of vision into needless, non productive, ill-fated discussions which will divert their attention and delay the completion of their task.

LOOK INSIDE

Remember, your dream starts with sound, not sight. Hearing is more important than seeing, for the eye is not as "keen" as your ability to listen. That's why you must learn to "see with your ears," not your eyes.

In the innermost parts of your being, your heart becomes tuned to what the Master is saying, then your eyes and hands begin to follow. You will never see with your natural eyes what the Master is preparing for your destiny. It is a Spirit-revelation, not a physical sighting. To fully embrace a Divine Plan, you must not develop a simultaneous fall-back plan. God never moves to "Plan B." He is a "Plan A-only" Creator. Trust Him.

This aspect of life is challenging because it causes you to look internally to discover how you process information and proceed when nothing is visible.

Yes, there are dark moments, but when a dreamer is in a "full-speed-ahead" mode he can still see. Why? Because dreams usually arrive in our subconscious, not while we are awake.

This is different from making plans since we usually do the latter in daylight. But the Almighty delivers our vision mainly while we are in a state of slumber.

THE "NIGHT FIGHT"

The Master knows how tempted we are to monitor achievement, choose the course and control the process of our success. Yet, He needs to be in full control.

Dreamers must relinquish their need for control. Our Father is in total charge. We need only to rest in Him and trust the plans He sets for our lives.

This is why God waits until our subconscious sleep arrives. Then, on the canvas of our minds and hearts, He begins to paint visions

There is something special about the night, for
when we desire rest, the Master desires greatness.
You want sleep and He wants productivity.

It is in the night hours when the Lord begins to overpower sleep to invade our minds. It's the "night fight" for position, and we must allow God to win without compromise.

YOUR SOURCE OF REST

When the Master is speaking, don't try to sleep, it's impossible. Not even warm milk, herbal teas or sedatives can silence His voice when it's time for a vision.

It is not uncommon for dreamers and visionary men and women to be alert and awake for an entire night, yet wake up actually energized—as if they had enjoyed eight hours of tranquil sleep.

Since the Master never slumbers, His specialty is rest, not sleep. He says, *"Come unto me, all ye that labor and are heavy laden, and I will give you rest"* (Matthew 11:28).

This is important because we can't comprehend the depth of His plans for us while we are burdened.

REGAINING CONFIDENCE

Rest is the state of being confident that nothing sent to or against us will override what is promised. Isn't it wonderful this is what God offers us when our burdens seem overwhelming?

We finally realize it is not our responsibility to bring the dream to pass. At rest, the believer becomes a servant of the Master, not a master to the situation. You will never control trials, tribulations or any event sent by the Father to make you strong.

Pacing the corridors of life is not an answer to rest, nor does it allow you to continue dreaming or to hear what God is saying concerning the next move.

Sleep is healthy, but not essential, when a dream is being unfolded. The person who insists, "I need my eight hours," is not a mature dreamer.

Rest is all you need, because when it is present, power and determination will follow. It is the means by which you begin to regain confidence over adversities.

HEART REVELATION

The condition of your heart will cause others to catch your vision and either work with or against you. This is why you need to give your heart a personal checkup. Beware, however, because not everything you find may be pleasant, and spiritual or emotional surgery may be required—with an extended stay in recovery.

Disappointments tend to find nesting places in our hearts and can remain dormant for years, even decades.

When these issues are not resolved they will manifest

themselves in various forms including sleep deprivation, weight disorders, inability to work with others, and even cause some to become team distractions rather than team builders.

David asked for a clean heart and a right spirit. In short, this was an internal makeover. Perhaps we should make a similar request.

Since the visionary heart is such a vital lifeline of a dreamer, stay focused, get your rest and remain patient.

A "seeing" dreamer is one who comprehends a promise through "heart revelation" and begins to move upon it long before the eye views what lies ahead. An example of this is the prophet Elijah who heard the sound of abundance of rain when there wasn't a cloud in the sky! (1 Kings 18:41).

Dreamers will learn to hear showers of blessing long before the skies open.

WHAT'S NEXT?

I enjoy music of all genres and have a vast collection. Years ago, my albums were stored in bulky cardboard boxes, then came eight track tapes and next, cassettes.

However, someone kept dreaming and decided vast amounts of music could be compressed into a CD. Another visionary believed we could digitize music and carry in excess of 5,000 songs in our shirt pocket or clipped to our hip—and along came the IPOD.

There is no telling what is next for the individual who clears his mind and heart of all debris and births something even more revolutionary.

BEYOND EMOTIONS

Your heart must be open to the Master's voice. However, be careful of being led by your compassionate emotions rather than your wisdom and intellect.

The Lord faced this from His disciples on several occasions including the feeding of 5,000 hungry men, women and children. After the people began complaining about not having any food, Philip told the Lord, "Eight months wages wouldn't be enough for each one to have a bite."

Then one of the disciples, Andrew, spoke up, *"There is a lad here, which hath five barley loaves, and two small fishes: but what are they among so many?"* (John 6:9).

We all know the story how the masses were fed with the "miracle lunch," but need to remember that initially, the disciples offered excuses rather than belief.

THE MUDDY WATERS

Unless we find people with vision, we will face Katrina-size disasters again and again. It wasn't the storm, rather the wrong team of responders which created the real disaster—not making the right decisions in a timely manner.

New Orleans and its countless families will forever be affected by this frailty. Likewise, metal detectors in airports did not stop 9-11, because the system is not designed, nor can it handle, the mind of terror.

When dreamers see these fault-lines, they will create new systems to make the world a safer place.

A UNITED VISION

I recently had to conduct a major restructuring of our ministry which required looking into the dark places of the hearts of my leaders who had been faithful for nearly ten years.

This task came at some turbulent moments where progress was constantly met with excessive delays and excuses. Some members were playing favorites with friends while others who appeared to support the ministry, actually sought a position to undermine the vision and destiny of its leadership.

As I viewed the organization, sadly, it became apparent that faithfulness was not sufficient enough reason to retain certain leaders.

When the qualities of contributions are no longer consistent with the vision it is incumbent upon the dreamer to exercise wisdom and make changes where necessary.

FAITHFULNESS VS. PRODUCTIVITY

Reorganization is both difficult and expensive in the world of ministry for you will be judged and criticized by the parties *being* changed and those *wanting* change. The latter group considers you to be negligent and untimely in making the decisions, while the former group will not acquiesce to the need for there removal.

In nearly thirty years of business ownership, management and ministry, I have never had an ill-equipped employee or volunteer willingly tender a resignation. The protest is pronounced when you confront such a person, for they never seem to want to make adjustments.

It is your duty to periodically evaluate those within your organization and determine their worth against the value of your God-given dream.

If an individual is no longer able to contribute effectively or make required change to become productive, you are responsible for making the decision for them.

The element of faithfulness is not to be confused with productivity—for not all faithful parties contribute to your mission or vision. It seems some are planted to undermine every goal and objective you set.

DREAMERS AND DISCORD

I urge you to learn a critical lesson from our Master's management style. Judas was with Him until the end, but He was only one of the twelve.

Dreamers or leaders must have an infrastructure which consists of followers who go beyond faithfulness. Judas was faithful until Calvary.

It is impossible to complete your assignment with twelve individuals like Judas, yet that person of discord will often provide you with the courage and tenacity to complete the task.

In this context, a "Judas" is valuable, since he forces you to remain committed and focused.

Dreamers and leaders must have an infrastructure which consists of disciples who understand more than vision and faithfulness. Those who are close need to know and protect your heart.

Discord is the byproduct of a faithful yet uncommitted, biased, jealous spirit which creates insubordination.

YOUR BIRTHRIGHT

There are dreamers who eventually become influential but will not understand this concept in the early stages of development because seldom do they know what is called "birthright." Also, they may not fully comprehend how others within their sphere may possess bitter hearts toward what God has placed within them.

I firmly suggest that dreamers quickly grasp the *right* of success which is provided by the Master.

Birthright suggests a position of inheritance, and also establishes order and respect. Hence, as a dreamer you need to know what the Master has declared over your life so you will not accept positions which are not productive to your future.

As indicated, seldom do dreamers find birthright without struggle or having the ability to hold onto a power or dream. For example, Jacob was able to live with the disappointment from his father-in-law because he knew the value of his birthright. It shapes desire—which in turn shapes patience and hope.

YOUR HEART'S DESIRE

When the dream is healthy, you will learn how to patiently work until it comes to fruition.

Let's not forget the story of Leah being given to Jacob as his wife instead of Rachel (Genesis 29). The latter was the dreamer's desire, and the former was his assignment. Yet, the process built character and fidelity.

———————— ⋀ ————————

Dreamers learn to fulfill duties, whether or not they are desirable.

Even if you express disappointment, don't allow your feelings to hold you in needless captivity for an extended period of time.

Jacob worked fourteen long years for a desire that was first promised to be his in seven years. Her name was Rachel.

Friend, your passion also has a name attached to it. If the assignment is not of your choosing you must realize God is working in this situation. Jacob expressed a willingness to work seven additional years because his heart's desire was still in reach.

A dreamer must carry a compass of life and a map for direction at all times. Focus is the compass and determination is the road map to complete the journey.

———————— ⋀ ————————

When in crisis, a dreamer should realize how to weather the storm without drowning.

If the apostle Paul could float to shore on the broken wreckage of a ship, why can't we survive by staying focused?

SOUND ADVICE

Learn how to effectively communicate with a trusted peer or leader. You see, most followers are less fortunate than yourself and will not provide you with sound advice during a turbulent situation.

I have a dear brother who is related in spirit, not through our natural blood line. Since he is a Floridian, he is very knowledgeable in giving direction in storms. Perhaps there is some reason for our love and admiration, for he knows hurricanes and I, as a Californian, know about earthquakes.

The communication we share is priceless as it brings each man value—whether one is in a hurricane or the other is in an earthquake. We are storm partners for life.

SILENCE AND OBEDIENCE

In biblical history, silence played a role on two special occasions. The first was when God told Joshua to have the armies of Israel walk around the walls of Jericho in complete silence for six days.

An entire army had to face an imposing obstacle—namely Jericho's wall—and possible humiliation. Yet, through their obedience and silence, God was able to move physical structures.

Since the enemy was fortified behind the wall and had the prime position against all of Israel, fighting them seemed impossible. However, the marching without speaking began to inspire belief in these soldiers. They were being prepared to occupy a place where hardship and struggle would cease.

If only dreamers could realize that past conflicts are

just those—past. They are no longer relevant to the future. Chalk them up as experience and reflect upon them without looking for another fight.

Quiet Submission

The second time silence played a key role was when our Master hung on Calvary and "opened not His mouth." There was tremendous suffering, public humiliation and sorrow which gave Him every right to express His displeasure, yet silence was essential to completing His assignment. Christ's submission to His Father opened the door to His ultimate victory.

Finally, looking up to heaven, He said, *"Father forgive them for they know not what they do"* (Luke 23:34).

In these transition points of life, permission to speak was denied. Victory came through silence, not a verbal exchange.

A Symbol of Strength

Human behavior is resistant to this change, for we move with memory and emotion which often seeks justification or retaliation.

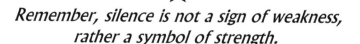

Remember, silence is not a sign of weakness, rather a symbol of strength.

Dreamers should find new strategies, other than to waste time with enemies who are soon to be destroyed.

Try controlling your tongue and watch how quickly your mind will come to rest. This will confuse your enemy who previously agitated you into needless, unorthodox behavior.

Possessing the will and ability to remain quiet is a crucial gift since it shows how near you are to making the transition to becoming a dreamer.

QUESTIONS WILL COME

It is not uncommon to experience a restructuring in your communication now that you are on to the path to becoming a Dream Walker. Not only will your style change, but the audience may be different when you begin to move into insightful positions of becoming what the Master has spoken into your life.

It can be an awkward feeling when those who previously understood and embraced you are now questioning every word and action. This may seem undeserving and painful since most visionaries are passionate, caring and nurturing individuals by nature.

A time will come when silence will be on your lips. Sure, you have much to pour out from the heart but your mouth is now mute.

No one in your immediate circle can seem to accept what is happening—for seldom will your conversations be understood by those who have not been chosen to walk with you during this change in your life.

It is at this juncture when you begin to feel manipulation or rejection.

A GUIDING HAND

Remain inspired by promise and never surrender

when peers are sent to distract you from the course. My heart goes out to men who cannot trust another—because a season of muddy waters will surely come and you will need someone to rescue you or send aid.

Not all visionaries have an innate ability to master silence or effective communication, but the Lord will always provide you with a teacher or counselor to navigate you through this transition.

There is a pathway to your destiny and having a helping hand to walk with you will make the journey rewarding.

Starting today, ask the Master to direct and guide your communications. Let Him be the One who gives you permission to speak.

CHAPTER 6

A FRIEND CALLED DETERMINATION

I clearly recall the days when I enjoyed a comfortable position with the aerospace giant Martin Marietta, now called Lockheed Martin—complete with benefits, opportunity and tenure. Yet, because of a dream that was bubbling inside me, I decided to leave this Fortune 500 firm to start my own company—E&I Systems Incorporated.

To say the response I received from friends and associates was "cool" is an understatement. Even my own family could not comprehend my decision, thinking only of the risks involved.

It was a lean start. My first contract with the Federal Aviation Administration just barely paid the operating expenses, and my car doubled as a mobile office—with files stored in the trunk! To make matters worse, my "partner" unexpectedly pulled out of the venture hours before the first contract purely because he didn't believe the operation would succeed.

He later asked that I give him part ownership as I opened satellite offices in Washington, DC, Virginia, and New Jersey. Like so many relationships, the partnership was in full force during the planning stages, but came to a dead stop in the "sacrifice" stage.

A VOICE INSIDE

I was constantly reminded of my "good position" with Martin Marietta—as if it would erase my dream. I still smile when I think of my eldest brother (who has now passed on) declaring me to be insane for giving up the life I had.

To be honest, it was difficult to stay focused during the slow start of my new enterprise because of the constant "background noise" of gloom and doom. It seemed no one in my circle understood my vision.

My friends during this season of life were my former fellow workers. Although we had a bond, we didn't share the same dreams.

Yes, there were moments when I questioned myself and wondered if I should shelve my plans and return to the comfort and security I had once known. But every time I seriously considered giving up, there was an inner voice encouraging me to press on. Time after time, my determination rose to the surface and I continued one more day.

ANOTHER CHAPTER?

With God's help, the enterprise grew and prospered. Then, after ten years of this successful operation, I heard the voice of the Master telling me to close this chapter of my life and enter into full-time ministry.

Admittedly, the prospect of walking away from a prosperous engineering practice was extremely difficult. And I confess I acted in disobedience by staying in business and delaying the transition much longer than God directed.

The paradox for dreamers is: we tend to hold onto our achievements as if there cannot be more than one success in a lifetime.

We should not become one dimensional or directed by the power of achievement versus the power of the Father's voice.

We need to be open and ready for the day when He reveals His ultimate desire for our lives.

SET IN STEEL

Giving up the presidency of a productive engineering firm with its benefits, influence, associations and potential is far more involved than simply changing jobs. The freedom of ownership and financial independence at a young age—or any age—is a weighty matter.

So how does a dreamer walk into the steps ordered by the Master when it requires total release from your comfort zone? Once again, you face the abandonment of friends who finally supported your business success, yet somehow refuse to endorse this transition.

My career plan was set in steel with no room for deviation. I would establish my own business, then practice law. It never included being a senior pastor in full time ministry or a motivational speaker in business, government and social circles.

A 52-Day Miracle

The fuel for success is accomplishment, so when a dreamer experiences moderate to major achievements, it is natural to continue the journey and reach for even higher goals. Yet, God may decide you need a new objective.

Nehemiah, a great leader in biblical times, experienced a major professional career change. If you read his story you'll learn how he was moved to "City Planning and Design" after a season of being a cup bearer for the king (Nehemiah 1:11).

Following God's orders, he left his easy position to fulfill the dream of restoring the walls of Jerusalem, a city which had been in ruins for nearly 90 years. In 52 days he accomplished one of the most ambitious rebuilding programs in recorded history. It happened because of his obedience to both the dream and the assignment.

The benefits of his willingness to follow God's direction impacted an entire culture.

If Nehemiah had stayed in his former position, Jerusalem would probably have remained in disrepair for centuries.

The Sting of Disappointment

We tend to foster relationships with pure hearts and noble intents, thinking our gift of dreaming will provide solace, wealth and hope to others. In short, dreamers are philanthropic, tending to want more for others than themselves.

Unfortunately, not all recipients are trustworthy and operating with integrity. You will often feel the sting of disappointment while you seek to help.

———————ʌ———————

All dreamers, including our Master, make extreme sacrifices as payment for becoming "more than a conqueror."

In this context, however, success shouldn't be misunderstood to represent tangible wealth, rather it speaks to the ability to continuously dream, even in the face of opposition.

As the Lord was hanging or a cross in pain, His task was to make provision of life through His death. And during His final hour, He became more determined than ever in completing His assignment.

THE COMMISSION COMES FIRST

We, too, cannot abandon our calling—even when we feel the personal anguish or endure extended periods of darkness.

It is natural to desire our own wishes, yet I have come to realize how the Master gives us a commission before He releases the desire. It arrives to us in the form of sacrifice.

Greatness and sacrifice work hand in hand. Each has

a distinguished quality we feel and admire, yet few are willing to pay the price to acquire success.

What matters most is inspiration—the constant voice of our Master and Creator.

He continues to inspire excellence, even when there is a lack of financial support.

Money is a measure or means by which we acquire goods and services. A dreamer never depends solely upon money, neither will he or she withdraw when it is absent.

Wealth is more important to a dreamer than money. The difference is: wealth is the internal value which cannot be measured. It is the force that moves a dreamer to the exclusion of money. Wealth prevails in adverse and friendless times.

GUARD YOUR MIND

Prior to the fall in the garden, man was an open-minded social being, void of prejudice or jealousy. He communed with God, and was living in a perpetual state of abundance.

An internal struggle took place as the original man forfeited his prestigious position by losing his determination to remain in an endless wealthy state of being. The serpent obviously released a trigger in his mind, causing Adam to think his own decisions were more important than the Creator's.

The dreamer must build a safety net or mental awareness so he will not be swayed by contentious voices—causing him to question his values, purpose and worth.

This erroneous, unsolicited advice is designed to topple you from your secure place. For those who listen to the whisperings of Satan, the recovery period is long, and some never regain their original vision.

A TRUE FRIEND

Thankfully, you have a new friend waiting to move you back to your purpose—one called "determination." This is a dreamer's prized possession and must not be treated carelessly.

In fact, a visionary may be without confidants or support, but if he remains "driven," he will find that determination becomes a true friend.

Those who lose this treasured possession will be weighed down by sorrow until they no longer have the will to move forward. A broken-hearted dreamer may lie by the wayside for a considerable period of time unless he or she comes to understand the power of a strong determination.

It is not the Master's desire to see His children in a non-productive, frail state.

A firm resolution is exhibited in your deeds rather than your speech, and is combined with an internal driving force which arises out of adversity.

It is also the power which transfers the dream from the heart to the hand—from a concept into reality. A vision without manifestation is like a discussion with no action.

Who Sets the Value?

The dream becomes activated when the visionary realizes this prize "gifting" has a worth far more than previously imagined. When this happens, he or she launches and energizes the concept or enterprise.

———————⫫———————

The value of a dream is established by the dreamer—not by any outside measuring stick or another's opinion.

The more determination we acquire, the higher the worth.

When a vision is abstract and without clarity, who can know where it will take you? But as it becomes defined and you are able to articulate it in precise terms, the value increases.

Since a true dreamer possesses uncommon qualities, the market place is ready to receive your gifts, talents, products and inspirations. What has been placed in your heart is divinely unique.

Success and Loneliness

To be honest, walking into your calling can quickly reduce the number of friends or associates within your life. Remember, there is a direct correlation between success and loneliness.

Certainly, relationships are critical to the circle of a dreamer, but a true visionary must never lose sight of the mission—even when it is no longer supported by your peers.

RIGHT RELATIONSHIPS

If you have spent time and energy trying to maintain friendships which turn out to be futile, don't feel guilty. It is our Father, the one who is closer than a brother, who is ultimately in control of our lives and we need to trust Him to bring about the right relationships.

When you concentrate on being friendly rather than seeking friends, you will begin to attract the quality of individuals who will be drawn to you because of the righteousness of your heart.

Without question, friendship is a precious commodity, yet dreamers must begin to have an even higher appreciation for right relationships—so that the loss of a friend will not destroy your vision.

In addition, make certain your understanding of "connections" is based on your divine relationship with the Master. Ask Him to direct you to those who possess the core beliefs and life principles necessary to establish a mutually beneficial alliance.

A TROWEL AND A SPEAR

When you read the story of Nehemiah, you'll see how people sought to impede his work as he began to make significant strides.

The construction was only half-finished when, *"Sanballat, and Tobiah, and the Arabians, and the Ammonites, and the Ashdodites, heard that the walls of Jerusalem were made up, and that the breaches began to be stopped, then they were very wroth, and conspired all of them together to come and to fight against Jerusalem, and to hinder it"* (Nehemiah 4:7-8).

The animosity became so hostile that the workers literally had to have a trowel in one hand and a spear in the other! The Bible records, *"They which builded on the wall [had] one of his hands wrought in the work, and with the other hand held a weapon"* (v.17).

No one cares about your God-directed project while it remains subjective or a random thought in your mind. They won't say a word while it is on the drawing board or the topic of idle conversation. But just start building and watch the fireworks!

This is when the opposition arises.

FINGERPRINTS ON THE WEAPON

You never know when or from where dissension will rear its ugly head, but having a conflict with a loved one is far worse than a disagreement with a stranger. When the arrows fly from those you have nurtured, fed, carried and cried with, it is a sad moment indeed.

What a tragedy to find their fingerprints on a weapon which seeks to shatter your dream. Unfortunately, this happens more often than we would like to admit.

Even among business, church and social associates, you will find dissenters would rather circumvent the process and sacrifice their friendship for a moment of temporary gain.

Let's be honest, not all of your friends share your desire. Some have a deficit of character or integrity and will use deceit to form an Absalom-like army with the intention of destroying both you and your promise (2 Samuel 13).

Since real dreamers are innocent—pure in spirit, mind, heart and soul—this can cause great anguish.

A FIRM FOUNDATION

As you progress in life and your dreams move to reality, there is usually a fork in the road that will separate those who support your vision from those who don't. Do not become discouraged when this happens because friendship is not a numbers game. I can tell you from personal experience, it's better to have ten friends who trust and believe in you than 100 who are along for the ride.

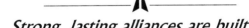

Strong, lasting alliances are built on common foundations, so make sure you are walking with like-minded people who love and respect your God-given vision.

THE ULTIMATE SOURCE

I've encountered people who have placed their inspired visions on hold for years, even decades, as they seek to recover from the pain of broken relationships in marriage, ministry and business ventures.

This is especially true for dreamers, since they are almost always heart-driven individuals and feel the loss deeply.

I encourage you to cherish every relationship, remembering the most treasured of all is the one which exists between you and your Heavenly Father. He is the ultimate source of your dreams and determination.

CHAPTER 7

FINDING YOUR DESIRE

Men often have a difficult time embracing a loving and caring concept such as "desire." It is an issue that seems "soft" because of the way we have been raised regarding true strength and manhood.

We are fearful of accepting the topics of dreaming and passion since the area has been erroneously linked to being weak or "less than a man."

However, sensitivity to the Master is not a gender preference, rather it is a wise choice.

How can you truly love the Lord with all of your heart, soul and mind if you do not know how to be in agreement with the *behavior* of God. Our Father desires *"...above all things that thou mayest prosper and be in health, even as thy soul prospereth"* (3 John 1:2).

Clearly, desire is not a word which lacks compassion.

HARNESSING STRENGTH

Recently, I have begun to introduce men to the value

of "sensitivity" as a means to harness strength and remove icy sterility from their lives. Instead of being a social negative, it is actually a divine application which allows you to see and hear all the Master has planned for you.

Sadly, insensitive and unemotional behavior has cast its long shadow over ministry, marriages, careers and social institutions. We have become a generation of wounded and bleeding dreamers, mistrusting spouses and, in some cases, reclusive visionaries.

As a result, a "cold" person may continue to operate in their gift, but eventually the ribbon holding the box together will fray causing them to resent friends, loved ones and assignments.

YOUR "INNER DRIVE"

The vast number of men and women are never taught how to move toward dreams, missions and relationships with the care and tender understanding of our Heavenly Father.

The need for passion and desire is misunderstood by those who have been instructed to be goal oriented to the absence of truth or feeling.

I am not suggesting that dreamers are characterless or illogical, but when you exclude "inner drive" from life, a dream or business venture it will either stagnate or die.

Those with a vision are passionate people and it is important to realize that not all listed in your biological chain or Rolodex of friends and associates will have the same love for your dream—but remember, it is the Master who gives it to you.

AN INTERNAL HUNGER

Life without desire is like a world without a sun, moon or stars. It is:

- The central core of you becoming all that has been spoken over and into your life.
- An internal hunger augmented by and an endless thirst for that which is specific in nature.
- A drive which takes what is abstract and begins to formulate it into something tangible with substance.

A HEALTHY OBSESSION

Desire has no point of settlement short of satisfaction, so it is not uncommon to find a person of 40-plus years becoming agitated due to some unfulfilled desire.

Since it is a self-motivating stream, it's almost impossible to dam its flow with alternate programs, business decisions, ministry assignments, constant shopping sprees or exotic vacations.

Dreaming is a behavior which is difficult to fully explain, but when desire takes complete control of your thoughts, the result is total success.

Even more, since true desire doesn't comprehend

limitations, it becomes an obsession or demand until the objective is met.

What we are discussing is not a condition which can be treated medically or through group therapy. It differs from burnout, but has similar symptoms. Burnout affects the actions of a dreamer, while desire stirs his passion.

CRYING FOR A TREAT

A child learns desire at a tender age—communicating it through finger-pointing and sound.

When a two-year-old cries to eat dessert instead of vegetables, the parent responds, "Not until you finish your meal."

The youngster hears the instruction, but mentally overrides it because of his longing for a treat. You've no doubt witnessed the process and watched a baby use his lips and tongue to spit out the vegetables until he gets what he craves.

My youngest daughter learned how to hold food in her mouth, as if she had eaten it. Only when I handed her the treat did I learn the messy truth!

THE BABY BOTTLE!

My eldest daughter had her moments, too. Once, on a trip to Connecticut, I decided she was old enough to give up drinking milk from a baby bottle. So I convinced her, "Pretty girls don't carry baby bottles."

The next thing I knew, she took her plastic bottle and threw it out of the car sunroof—and with the sweetest voice repeated, "Pretty girls do not carry bottles."

Little did I know her desire for a bottle was to be

short lived. So about 1:30 A.M. I lost the battle and left a warm bed searching for an open store to buy a replacement baby bottle on a cold, cold New England night.

Once again, desire won!

THE EXIT PLAN

The symptoms of lost passion can be documented by listing the number of projects a person starts but never finishes.

What causes the delay? Is it fear? Self-sabotage? A discouraging word from someone you love?

Since one excuse is as good as another, we must find a way to recapture the passion we once had and continue to press ahead. It makes no difference what others think.

Our destiny is revealed to our hearts by the Father and we will disappoint Him—and ourselves—if we fail to act upon the dream.

Since desires can be either evil or pure, you must ask God to help you as you journey on the road of righteousness.

A Dream Walker will not only encounter dead end paths, he must learn how to anticipate them and prepare an exit plan.

PITFALLS FOR A PURPOSE

It is not unusual for a dreamer to experience what I call the "emptiness of life syndrome."

Perhaps you, like me, have faced times when it seemed there was no way out. You tried to pray, yet there was no immediate answer. Prayer gave you strength, but the negative situations did not change.

------------**⚊⚊⚊⚊**------------

Don't blame God needlessly. Like the valley He allowed Job to walk through, the pitfalls are for a purpose.

The Master will sustain you through the bleakest hours because He knows what lies ahead.

"I WILL FIND IT"

Life can be derailed without a moment's notice.

I think of Katrina's hurricane victims who knew a storm was coming, yet weren't faced with the reality until the winds subsided. That's when the levees broke and the city was flooded. Through media coverage we witnessed the faces of exhausted men, women and children who were bewildered and disoriented.

However, in story after story, people were clinging by their fingernails to the bare threads of desire. One woman, with tears streaming down her cheeks, said, "If there is anything to live for, I will find it!"

One of the images that will never be erased from my memory was a New Orleans teenager who commandeered a local school bus and drove dozens of people to higher ground, hundreds of miles away.

He had no license or driving experience, yet this thing

called "desire" caused him to help those in need to escape the jaws of death.

However, for most of us, our foe is not a violent storm which inflicts mass destruction, rather a quiet, empty feeling of hopelessness which gnaws away at our spirit day after day, month after month. This silent killer, if not managed, will have the same devastating effect.

INCREASING THE VALUE

In every arena of life, man's desire makes the difference.

As an art collector I have come to realize that the value of an artist's work rises when what he or she expresses on canvas totally arrests your attention.

Artists who can mentally transport you to another place or time and have you admire and gaze endlessly at a canvass, have captured your desire. At that moment, the price you are willing to pay for this work increases.

For today's young generation, Hip Hop music has become an artistic expression—it's their Mona Lisa.

The lyrics may be lacking in tenderness, yet this evolution in lifestyle somehow serves a passion few over 40 understand.

AN ESSENTIAL ALIGNMENT

The moment dreamers move into God's desire for their future, they will find an endless reservoir of possibilities. Why? Because they are suddenly in harmony with the will of the Master.

This alignment is essential since not all desires are prudent, healthy or beneficial. For this reason, visionaries must possess a discerning spiritual "decoder" so they won't make wrong choices or bad decisions which are satisfying today but destructive tomorrow.

AN "INTERNAL BURN"

Opposition never comes when you walk away from a vision, it only appears and presents its pain when the Dream Walker begins to complete or finish an inspired task.

Surrendering prematurely to something less than your passion will never satisfy the longing or "internal burn" for which your heart craves.

A PASSIONATE WORSHIPER

It's easy to categorize King David as a dreamer, yet he had a difficult time overcoming his past and making the transition.

He suffered from unresolved rejection and social acceptance. As a young man he was wounded by his earthly father, Jesse—who lied to Samuel when he implied he had no more sons. David had lived in shattered silence, admitting, *"I was shapen in iniquity, and in sin did my mother conceive me"* (Psalm 51:7).

He eventually found comfort in the Master's love, yet he could not find solace in his own house. Those close to him were even embarrassed at his public expressions of dancing unto the Lord (2 Samuel 6).

In Psalm 27, David addresses the emotional

"drought" he was going through—and the answer he found: *"When my father and my mother forsake me, then the Lord will take me up"* (v.10).

Here, he is no longer the messenger, shepherd or musician who attempts to soothe Saul, but is now a passionate worshiper seeking the presence of God.

David writes, *"One thing have I desired of the Lord, that will I seek after; that I may dwell in the house of the Lord all the days of my life, to behold the beauty of the Lord, and to inquire in his temple. For in the time of trouble he shall hide me in his pavilion: in the secret of his tabernacle shall he hide me; he shall set me up upon a rock"* (vv.4-5).

A SHEPHERD'S HEART

David is perplexed to learn that humanity is not like the sheep he tenderly cared for on the hillsides.

Sheep just want direction, food and water and protection from predators. They understand the nudge of the shepherd's staff is for their safety—and when they stray it takes just one tap to have them return to the fold.

Yet, this innocent young man with a shepherd's heart rose to the place of a king and learned that life could be cruel. This is why he turned to the Lord for consolation and comfort.

"RENEW A RIGHT SPIRIT"

A prerequisite of a God-ordained desire is that we become internally truthful and monitor our heart. David addressed this issue by saying, *"Behold, thou desirest truth in the inward parts: and in the hidden part thou shalt make me to know wisdom"* (Psalm 51:6).

Read David's deep desire: *"Hide thy face from my sins, and blot out all mine iniquities. Create in me a clean heart, O God; and renew a right spirit within me. Cast me not away from thy presence; and take not thy holy spirit from me. Restore unto me the joy of thy salvation; and uphold me with thy free spirit"* (Psalm 51:9-12).

The inward search for truth germinates yearnings that are pure and healthy. This is not for group discussion, rather for the dreamer himself who is ready to move into a great task, complete a ministry assignment, launch a business venture or take a turn for the better in his personal life.

THE "SNAKE LINE"

Change is temporary, but when it is combined with desire, it becomes both an evolutionary—even *revolutionary*—process where you no longer can return to previous weakness, failures, pains, and disappointments.

You are embracing what a friend calls "the snake line of transformation." This is a height where the air is so thin that serpents turn and head for lower ground.

Mountain climbers don't have to carry snake repellent since it's not necessary at this elevation.

In life, the "conflict line" is low and filled with harmful, adverse elements. But the "desire line" is always at a level far higher than the norm—above disappointments, character assaults and major altercations.

Let me encourage you today to receive a passionate

vision which is above the snake line of your life.

WHO WILL WIN?

Experiences such as personal rejection, an unsuccessful business venture or a failed marriage are certainly life-altering events, but they can become distant memories when the internal pull of a fresh vision and a new mission is present.

——————⋀——————

Conflicts will clash with your desire, but you need to ask yourself, "Who will win?"

The reason you will be victorious is because as a dreamer your drive and passion is no longer subject to your environment. In fact, it's just the opposite.

Your divine gift is alive, waiting for you to finish that which has come under attack.

Now is your time to triumph!

CHAPTER 8

START WALKING!

After every major event of creation, the Master announced: "And it was so!"

These four simple words contain a powerful truth because they express the "completeness" of a dreamer. They are a proclamation from the Almighty of both you and your vision.

Don't be overly concerned about the time which may have elapsed between the initial dream and this moment. God gave the vision for a purpose and as long as His voice continues to lead and guide, it's still yours.

Your aspirations are not a byproduct of your imagination, rather a direct creation of His commandment. In the Master's sight, your success is no longer optional, but mandatory.

THE VIEW FROM ABOVE

We must learn to agree with the path we are given, even if the direction may at first seem undesirable. The journey is not chartered to our standards or choices, it is God's plan of success placed into our mortal minds.

It began, and will continue to be, *His* dream, and we have a duty to carry it forward.

We only have a limited picture based on our hopes and desires, yet the clearest view is seen from above.

Life is no longer a question of "Should I enter into the place God has prepared?" Instead, ask yourself, "Why wait another moment?" It is time and you are prepared to walk into your dream.

How you are going to travel there? Hopefully, it will be by chariot rather than a wheelchair!

SOMETHING MORE

There is one component of the process which may be missing.

Over the course of life, many dreamers establish a defense mechanism in their character which prohibits others from getting too close to them and finding out who they are and what values they possess.

In Chapter One I spoke of my childhood when I used toy soldiers for protection. Yet, in my current season of living, it would raise more than a few eyebrows if I began an important board meeting, a seminar or a contract negotiation by lining up plastic soldiers on the conference table as a shield of safety.

The painful memories of past mistakes, failed marriages, dysfunctional relationships, difficult people, financial hardships and prevailing mental wars are your prime excuses for becoming isolated and closing the doors to the future.

CELEBRATE YOUR ACCOMPLISHMENTS

What is the missing link which will allow you to walk into your dream? A God-ordained relationship.

You must attach your heart and soul to a "called" individual who sees beyond what you alone can visualize. He or she has been given to you by the Master for the purpose of walking with you into the greatest season of your life. In fact, it may be more than one person.

God has gloriously shaped your thoughts and determination, and now you are on the verge of victory. He is using others to be at your side—even if they may not know your past.

Trust the Father to send new individuals to pursue a relationship with you who have no hidden agendas or impure motives. You will know who they are—people who desire nothing more than your trust and confidence.

They are sent to walk with you into your dreams and celebrate your accomplishments. Let them become part of your achievement by saying, "And it was so!"

TAKE THE RISK

It may be difficult to believe there are such outstanding men and women waiting to accompany you on the road called Triumph.

This is a very brave moment for a dreamer, because it requires more trust than intellect, and more heart than head. Remember, our thoughts are not always willing to forget past injustices and allow another being into our innermost space. We are afraid to risk additional setbacks, yet we *must* accept this assignment of relationship before obtaining the dream.

A wounded visionary can become his or her worst enemy because the level of trust or number of relationships they allow to develop are few—if any.

Finding the right confidant is not a finger-walking trip through the Yellow Pages. Rather, he or she will appear as a direct result of your prayerful desire and wise counsel.

Let His Spirit guide you. For example, you should not blindly take advice from a person who admittedly is envious of your position. Neither should you seek the ear of an individual who is noticeably weaker in character or lacks integrity.

BUILD THE TRUST

Right relationships are rare to come by, yet they are priceless and must be protected while on this final leg of your journey.

Logical minds conclude the ideal person should come from a member of your family, but we know this is often far from reality. In truth, as a dreamer, you may experience strong rejection from those who either possess your bloodline or are jealous of your God-given talents.

How do you determine such a bond is appropriate for this season? There are some clear indicators, yet you must first admit that relationships for you are difficult.

If this is true, go ahead and confess your shortcomings regarding making friends. This hesitancy is understandable since as a dreamer you possess such keen abilities and qualities that the effort of building a trustworthy friend may seem cumbersome or a waste of valuable time.

However, settle this issue quickly and move forward to building this necessary trust with another individual.

It is at this point you are entering the "home stretch" of the miracle marathon.

FORGET YOUR FOES

Another biblical truth relates to those who are against you and may even be plotting your defeat. Instead of seeking revenge or wishing them ill will, take time to pray for them. As the Psalmist reminds us, *"Thou preparest a table before me in the presence of mine enemies"* (Psalm 23:5).

Thank God, He rarely presents more than one Red Sea crossing in a generation. He will take care of your enemies in the angry waters, allowing you to cross safely onto dry ground.

ANTICIPATE THE PRIZE

The price of achievement is found in the heart, not in the balance sheet of an investment account. Dream Walkers understand and respect money, yet they are not single-minded and know how to continue moving forward without dwelling on funds.

An idea is not considered valuable because of the financial status of its creator, rather because of the inspiration and "sales force" behind the dreamer.

The average person who suffers a financial setback questions his self worth. However, a Dream Walker forges ahead in lean seasons as if nothing has been lost. He is secure in knowing what will come has higher value than what has been destroyed or removed.

Don't take an inventory of what was taken; begin to anticipate the prize just ahead!

"WHAT'S NEXT?"

I believe you have read this book for a purpose and I am praying you will begin to walk into the most rewarding days of your life:

- Your marriage will become what your heart has desired.
- Your ministry will now unfold into what your prayers have painted.
- Your career or business enterprise will succeed above and beyond anything you imagined.

The Master saw in you what others failed to realize—that you were a possessor of "birthright knowledge" and your greatest resources, inspiration and determination were housed in your mind and heart.

You have weathered storms and disappointments while staying focused and true to your mission.

Because your wealth resided in your vision, financial favor is finding you. Others may not understand, but the mystery is beginning to unfold.

The sound principles within you that were previously dormant have been awakened and you are making significant strides.

You are no longer bothered by the cost since you would pay any price to see the dream reach reality.

You are now walking side by side with your desires and there is a passion for life which satisfies you from within. Craving external approval is no longer your priority.

As a Dream Walker, you are determined to complete everything the Master has said concerning you and your future. No longer are you asking, "Can it be?" Instead you are waiting with eager anticipation, wondering, "What's next?"

THE PRINCIPLES

By allowing the message on these pages to come alive in your heart, mind and soul, you will begin to enter into and enjoy God's riches and abundance planned from the day you were born.

Here's a recap of just a few of the principles we've discovered:

- Looking back is essential, but going back is *deadly!*

- The true measure of success is not assessed by the neighbor next door, rather by the gift within.
- As you begin planting, it is essential to focus on the seed, not the entire crop.
- When unconditional trust is combined with belief, all things are possible.
- Allow rejection to bring you into total surrender to the Master, not to mankind.
- There is a direct correlation between the number of setbacks and the value of your dream.
- Those who place you in a pit must not be seen as your enemies, but agents of change leading you to a higher position.
- Problems are not impossibilities unless you seek to solve them alone rather than ask for your Master's help.
- It is far more serious to be mentally crippled than physically disabled.
- The past must be viewed as a foundation on which failure can be built into success.
- Your dream starts with sound, not sight. That's why you must learn to "see with your ears," not your eyes.
- Focus is the dreamer's compass and determination his road map.
- Silence is not a sign of weakness, rather a symbol of strength.
- A firm resolution is exhibited in your deeds rather than your speech.

- It is better to have ten friends who trust and believe in you than 100 who are along for the ride.
- The Master will sustain you through the bleakest hours because He knows what lies ahead.

In the words of the Master Dreamer:

"For I know the thoughts that I think toward you, saith the Lord, thoughts of peace, and not of evil, to give you an expected end."
JEREMIAH 29:11

The toy soldiers are gone
You survived the pits, prisons and palace
Sickness came as did the crippling experiences
Lame excuses are no longer present
The value of your dream is worth living
— and live you shall
Walk my fellow dreamer, walk into your dream.

Your days of waiting and wanting are over. Start walking!

NOTES

FOR A COMPLETE LIST OF RESOURCES OR
TO SCHEDULE ANDREW C. TURNER II
FOR A "DREAM WALKER SEMINAR"
OR OTHER SPEAKING ENGAGEMENTS,
CONTACT:

ACT 2 PRODUCTIONS - MINISTRIES
425 SOUTH LA BREA AVENUE
INGLEWOOD, CALIFORNIA 90301

PHONE: 310-330-5500
INTERNET: www.dream-walker.com